Education, Technology, and Paradigms of Change for the 21st Century

To Mike,
With warmest regards,
David Thornburg

St. Charles High School
Resource Center
St. Charles, IL 60174

David D. Thornburg, Ph.D.

Starsong   Publications

Thornburg, David D.
Education, Technology, and Paradigms of Change for the 21st Century

ISBN 0-942207-09-2 (pbk.)
Copyright © 1989, 1991 by David D. Thornburg and Starsong Publications

All rights reserved. No part of this publication may be reproduced, stored in a retrieval system, or transmitted, in any form or by any means, electronic, mechanical, photocopying, recording, or otherwise, without the written permission of the publisher. Printed in the United States of America.

ISBN 0-942207-09-2
1 2 3 4 5 6 7 8 9 0

Dedicated to those who provide support and guidance as we jointly explore the infinite world of ideas –

Our quest has just begun...

Much learning does not teach understanding.
Heraclitus

Only the educated are free.
Epictetus

The mind is a fire to be kindled, not a vessel to be filled.
Plutarch

Teachers don't need to be fire kindlers, they need to become arsonists.
Ian Jukes

Give a little love to a child, and you get a great deal back.
John Ruskin

One's mind, once stretched by a new idea, never regains its original dimensions.
Oliver Wendell Holmes

Education enables individuals to come into full possession of all their powers.
Dewey

The empires of the future are the empires of the mind.
Winston Churchill

Knowledge is the most democratic form of power.
Alvin Toffler

To dream anything that you want to dream. That is the beauty of the human mind. To do anything that you want to do. That is the strength of the human will. To trust yourself to test your limits. That is the courage to succeed.
Bernard Edmonds

We learn wisdom from failure much more than from success; we often discover what will do, by finding out what will not do; and probably he who never made a mistake never made a discovery.
Samuel Smiles

Perhaps what we call genius has something to do with a learned state of consciousness, a way of attending to the stream of mental experience. Perhaps many more of us could hear inner melodies, find guidance and inspiration, achieve breakthrough insight – if we would only pay more attention to the fleeting images and the quiet intuitions presented to us by the creative mind.
Willis Harman

The starting point of all achievement is desire. Keep this constantly in mind. Weak desires bring weak results, just as a small amount of fire makes a small amount of heat.
Napoleon Hill

Education is not the filling of a pail, but the lighting of a fire.
William Butler Yeats

Carpe diem. (Seize the day.)

Contents

Introduction	7
Paradigm Paralysis and Educational Computing in the 21st Century	9
The Medium and the Message	15
Fragmented Education	20
Taking Chances	25
Technology and the School of the Future	30
Microworlds and Macroworlds	35
The Role of Technology in Teaching to the Whole Child	40
CD-ROMS and Educational Computing	70
Video Games and Informal Education	82
The Hacker Mentality in Education	89
Kid's Computing Comes of Age	93
Computers and Testing	99
Renaissance II – an Afterword	105
Glossary of Multimedia Terms	112
References	143

Introduction

Leonardo da Vinci was not only one of the world's greatest inventors, he was one of the most frustrated men to have ever lived. I think that much of his frustration came from the fact that he could think of technologies that, given the knowledge of the time, could not be built. His invention of the helicopter, for example, needed the internal combustion engine to make it work, and this engine would not be invented until many centuries later.

I mention this because we are at a wonderful period in the history of ideas and technology as these subjects relate to the restructuring of public education. We have, for one of the few times in history, a convergence of pedagogical thought and technological breakthroughs that fit like a hand in a glove. Research on multiple intelligences, the psychology of optimal experience, and the functioning of the human brain dovetail with the rapid development of inexpensive multimedia workstations and development systems in ways that can let any educator transform education for the benefit of all children.

These breakthroughs have come at a time of rapid change, and they come at a time when we are losing hundreds of thousands of students each year – dropouts who will be virtually unemployable in the next century.

I have several biases that need to be shared with you at this point. First, I think that a major goal of education should be the development of lifelong learners. Furthermore, I believe that each child comes to us with the capacity for total engagement with learning, and that this engagement can be maintained by allowing students to be constructors of their own knowledge.

I also believe that the technology so commonplace to our homes belongs in our classrooms as well. Universal access to computers, for example, is a theme that runs through the following pages.

The contrast between my vision (which probably is close to your vision as well,) and the reality of most classrooms is quite stark. I believe that each of us can become an agent for positive change, and I hope the following ideas provide food for thought as you work with your community of students, parents, colleagues, and the public at large.

The material in these chapters is largely derived from articles I've published in A Plus and inCider through my Learning Curve column. They are self-contained and can be read in any order you wish. Where appropriate, these articles have been condensed, expanded, and/or updated. Of course, the curse of any technology book is that it is out of date the day it hits the market. My hope is that the ideas I've presented outlast any specific references that have been rendered obsolete by the latest announcements from industry.

My goal is to stimulate your own thinking. Thank you for letting me share my views with you!

Paradigm Paralysis and Educational Computing in the 21st Century

As we enter the last decade of the 20th century, change continues to assume global proportions, as it will for the foreseeable future. While change is coming slowly to education, business is transforming itself with great rapidity just to stay alive.

External changes – the decline of our aging manufacturing base, the rise of the service sector, global transformations – mask more fundamental changes that strike to the very heart of all of us.

To a large extent these changes have been facilitated by technology. For example, the almost universal access to inexpensive solar-powered calculators has eliminated the mechanical slide rule on the engineer's belt; and, if we wanted it to, these calculators would change the way we teach mathematics to children of all ages.

Now that computers have become indispensable desk accessories, we can see the forces that have set in motion the next phase of our technological development.

Newton's paradigm
The 19th century industrial model that provided the foundation for our industrial growth was connected to a prevailing paradigm based on Newtonian physics – the notion that, like a falling body, the movement of

markets could be predicted and that business would be attracted to the strong center provided by the industrial giants.

Education was generally thought of as the filling of a vessel. The scope of a subject could be quantified and the student's mastery could be measured by "squeezing the sponge" and measuring what came out. The learner was, otherwise, a passive participant in the process.

This approach didn't cause too many problems at the time because a solid base of factual knowledge coupled with the ability to write and perform calculations was all that was needed for a lifetime job with a single employer.

As the 20th century developed, we underwent a revision in our model of the universe in which Newton's ideas broke down on close inspection. Einstein's notion of mass as energy, Bohr's ideas on the duality of waves and particles, and Heisenberg's principle regarding the inherent uncertainty of quantum events all forever destroyed the clockwork universe epitomized by classical physics.

Quantum shifts in technology

This paradigm shift in physics is finally being reflected in our lives. Technology, of course, is making this transformation possible, but it is the shift in our perspective that is critical. To see this, imagine a quantum experiment in which a photon (light particle) is directed to a diffraction grating. When it hits the grating, it behaves like a wave and is sent off in a new direction. Our traveling photon may then hit a photocell where it will be detected as a particle. Depending on its interaction with other objects, the photon can behave like a wave or like a particle.

Now take a look at modern communication using a fax machine. The document starts in one office in particle form (a sheet of paper). It is then placed on the fax machine where its information is then sent as electronic signals (waves) to the receiving machine on which it then reappears as a physical sheet of paper (in particle form.)

Contrast this form of communication with the older Newtonian pure particle model in which a letter is placed in an envelope and is sent through the mails. As the cost of carrying physical mail has increased, the cost of electronic transmission has decreased, making the new paradigm less expensive than the old one. For example, with today's postal rates, it is cheaper to fax a short document coast to coast than it is to mail it. As a side benefit, a message can be faxed halfway around the world in less than a minute. As millions of inexpensive fax machines are being purchased every year, the Newtonian Postal Service is in real risk of losing its high profit First Class mail to this electronic technology.

Another characteristic of the new physics is that time, space and matter coexist and interrelate to each other in subtle ways. From the perspective of relativity theory, we can see the office in a new light. Many thousands of people have decided that their office is wherever they are. Airplane cabins have been turned into airborne offices. Some people are listening to recorded courses on goal achievement while others are working with their laptop computers and still others are on the telephone. The home office now exists at 30,000 feet and is moving at close to the speed of sound.

Shouldn't a similar idea be reflected in our schools? Computers need to be where children are, and children need to be wherever learning takes place best. For some activities the classroom is perfect. For others, the library, zoo, or forest would be more appropriate. But for learning to take place in any environment, the modern tools of learning (such as calculators and computers) need to be with the learner, not locked away in a lab somewhere.

The success of the laptop computer market has had less to do with technology than with attitudes. The original personal computer of the 1970's was personal in ownership but not in use. The computer sat on a desk, not in our immediate possession. Today's laptops and notebook machines are truly personal. They can be used at a desk, or while sitting under a tree. True, some laptops (such as the Macintosh portable) are a bit on the hefty side, but, as computers like the $250 Laser PC-4 demonstrate, we are approaching a time when truly functional computing power will be within both the economic and physical reach of everyone.

In thinking about the future impact of technology in your life, think less about the hardware and more about the prevailing paradigms of physics.

Schools of the 90's
What impact do these paradigms have for education? Tragically, the impact to date has been very small. Most schools are in the 19th century backwaters of technology, relying on chalk and pens while kids' bedrooms have televisions, computers and CD players.

Even at this late stage in their development, classroom computers are still often seen only as boxes to run fixed applications, rather than as vehicles with which we can extend and expand our thinking.

As for placing computers in the hands of each child for use in the "anywhere, anytime" paradigm of 20th century physics, many reject the suggestion that we should just give this technology to children – even though it would cost less than 1% of the projected costs for bailing out the savings and loan crisis. I think this resistance comes more from a fear of change than for financial reasons.

Paradigm paralysis is commonplace, but its effects can be devastating. The nation that flocked to oat bran in response to a study conducted with only 250 patients still can't accept the benefits of educational technology, even though the benefits are being shown every day with hundreds of thousands of students.

The clock is ticking its way to 2001. We have about ten years to restructure education for the twenty-first century. As a user of personal computers, you can help others understand the benefit of this technology in extending students' ability to explore the space of concepts and ideas.

Break through paradigm paralysis and make this the year that universal access to technology is brought to all the students and staff at your school!

The Medium and the Message

The Canadian philosopher Marshall McLuhan spent many years exploring ways in which our media of expression influence the ideas we express. There is a world of difference between reading a newspaper for 10 minutes and watching a televised news broadcast for the same period of time. The newspaper reader is free to pick and choose, to skim or reflect. These freedoms are lost to the viewer of a television program, even though the animated visual medium lends itself to covering material that would be more difficult to convey in printed form. My reason for mentioning this is not to suggest that one medium of expression is somehow better than another, but rather that each medium has its own expressive power and that this power may better suit the needs of some people than others.

As we look at the computers gracing our classrooms, we might ask what messages are best communicated through this medium?

Computers are designed primarily to accept mechanical input (keyboard, joystick, touch tablet, etc.) and to provide visual and (to a lesser extent) auditory output. As a medium of communication it is closer to writing and drawing than it is to using a telephone, for example. (Although this distinction becomes fuzzy when the computer is connected to a bulletin board system through a modem.)

If we accept this model of computer interaction with the user, then all the communication takes place through the software. This is an area of tremendous flexibility. Provided that information can be captured through mechanical means and can be expressed visually, there is virtually no limit to the uses of computers. In the educational domain this means that computers can, in principal, be used for all subjects that involve written input and visual output. None of this is new; we've known this for over a decade now.

Since this model also applies to virtually all subject areas taught in a traditional manner, it is surprising that computers have yet to move into the educational mainstream. The flexibility of interaction between the user and the computer allows these tools to be used in ways that move far beyond the limitations of traditional lecture- and book-based delivery. These additional features, when combined with the traditional base of capabilities that characterize educational computing, should have resulted in an overwhelmingly positive response from the educational establishment.

And yet it hasn't.

Yes, over 2 million computers are now in schools, but this hardly scratches the surface. Furthermore, of these scant millions of machines, very few of them are being used to their greatest potential. Many computers are being used for supplemental activities, most of which can be conducted just as well from traditional workbooks.

As heartened as I am by the many thousands of teachers I see each year who are using classroom computers in wonderful ways, the great majority of today's educators have little interest in classroom computing. An unfortunate consequence of this disinterest is that these teachers, many of whom are tremendously effective, are assuming that the quality of their instruction can't benefit from exposure to new technology. We need to examine the role of technology as a tool that can help us teach to the whole child.

Those of you reading this book are most likely among the "early adopters" who've been using computers for years. If you fall in this category, you've seen a lot of software – both good and bad. But you've also seen some subtle shifts as computer technology is becoming connected with other media – laser video disks, CD-ROMs, etc.

In your hands, the classroom computer has become an expressive tool for discovery and true learning. In the process of finding your own best way to approach technology you've also found something else of great importance – that the only limitation to the use of this tool is your own imagination.

I believe that some people in the educational establishment are stalling so they don't have to confront a basic truth – deep down they are afraid to rethink the educational process. Yes, I know how seemingly expensive computer equipment can be, but history has shown us that, when our backs are against the wall, we can create excellent educational programs that reach across all grades, states, and economic levels; and that the money can suddenly materialize. What frustrates me is that, if history is our guide, it will be another country who is responsible the next major overhaul of our educational system.

If you doubt this, just look at the past. Prior to the Russian launch of Sputnik there were many highly regarded educators and visionaries who were trying to interest schools in new math and science programs, largely to no avail. But, within days of the Russian launch, improved education in this country became a major focal point for many prominent leaders. Why do we have to wait for some external event to blast us into action when all the resources and incentives for transformation are staring us squarely in the face?

The lethargy regarding education is phenomenal. Yes, there are many who speak out on this topic in an attempt to effect some change. Working at the grassroots level, I know many teachers who have created marvelous learning environments with their own sweat, tears and money. And still the public response is to engage in more hand-wringing and teacher bashing because it is always simpler to blame others than it is to effect change.

One of the things I love about educational computing in the past 10 years is the number of mistakes we've made. If you aren't failing part of the time, you probably aren't exploring new ground. We've seen pedagogically putrid software climb to the top of the charts while exquisite environments like Logo languish because many educators misunderstood the true power of this language. Some critics of educational computing use the lack of "documented" value as an excuse to constrain teachers to the awesome power of a sheet of slate and a stick of chalk.

The time has come for those of us who care deeply about education to join forces and to speak with a clear voice. We need to rededicate ourselves to our most noble purpose. Yes, children may represent 25% of our population, but they are 100% of our future. The society of today has no room for students who have been failed by a system that does not understand the fundamental difference between learning and teaching.

We must go back to the root of education – to draw out – and realize that we have invented marvelous tools designed to help draw out the true love of learning that I believe lies deep within each of us. Whether it is a history student creating a hypermedia database connected to a visual library of historical events, a fledgling composer crafting her compositions with a rack full of MIDI-based synthesizers, or a poet whose choice of typeface is made with as much care as the choice of words, today's computers are up to the task. It is vision that is lacking.

To the extent that money is an issue, we must demand that education be properly funded and, until such time as this funding is received, we must be on the lookout for sources of money to fund the software and hardware that can move at least some of our dreams closer to reality.

Fragmented Education

One of the byproducts of the assembly line model of education is the creation of a fiction with tremendous negative impact – the idea that knowledge can be divided into neat distinct classifications called "subjects". Each of these subjects (math, history, language arts, etc.) is often presented as if it were isolated from other subjects. It is as if education has gathered up the fabric of human existence and shredded it into small pieces with no hint as to how the student is to reassemble these parts into the wholeness of life.

Fortunately there are some educators who realize the danger of this artificial separation, and these teachers go out of their way to make sure that meaningful interrelationships are pointed out to students whenever possible. For example, an astute biology teacher might have students examine the spiral pattern on pine cones. Each cone has two sets of spirals running in opposite directions. By counting the spirals in each direction, students might find that one cone has 3 left handed spirals and 5 right handed ones. Still other cones might have 5 left and 8 right spirals. This biology teacher might then have the students notice that the two numbers they find are adjacent Fibonacci numbers from the series 1, 1, 2, 3, 5, 8, 13, etc. Furthermore, the students might discover that the ratio of these number pairs approaches the Golden Mean as the numbers get large. Other spiral patterned plants such as sunflowers and artichoke hearts could be used to extend this study, bringing the beauty of mathematics into the study of biology.

Activities of this type help to heal the rift of an educational process that is reflective of a philosophy of separation. The excitement that comes for student and teacher alike when such activities are introduced reflects the joy of healing a wound that has been open for over a century.

Current educational buzz-words such as "whole language approach" reflect an attempt to rebuild a holistic framework for knowledge. Fortunately, unlike the fate of Humpty Dumpty, we can put the pieces together again – and the computer can be our ally in the creation of an integrated "systems" approach to learning.

Traveling with computers

Several years ago I had the pleasure of visiting Venice where I spent hours photographing the floor of St. Mark's Cathedral. If that seems like a strange way to spend time, you need to know that I love geometry, and the tile patterns on that floor are spectacular!

As I looked at these intricate geometrical wonders, I wished I had some students with me. We could travel through Italy studying history, art, mathematics, science and music without having to think about where one subject started and one ended. I had visions of us with our laptop computers, sitting on the plaza outside the cathedral using Logo to recreate the tile patterns we'd seen. Other students would be capturing their impressions of the city in poetry while still others would be creating a historical database on the Renaissance. On their return home, these students would then create and present a multi-media presentation on their trip that would end up teaching all they had learned to those who hadn't been able to be there in person.

No excuses
The adventure I described isn't available to most students, but this is no reason to abandon the underlying idea. Any teacher with a computer and a desire to create an integrated educational program can do it. The rich variety of software available today is limited only by the imagination of the educator in its ability to make education whole again.

For example, suppose you are a teacher who is exploring California for social studies. One way to do this is to present the students with material right from the textbook. This familiar approach takes a fascinating topic and makes it boring. It causes some students to say, "Who cares?"

On the other hand, in the same period of time, a teacher who really cares about the subject may try a different approach. After exploring California's location on the planet and talking about the geologic upheavals that created some of the spectacular landscape, the students might be encouraged to imagine themselves as members of an ancient tribe of Indians, the Ohlones, for example. Student research on this tribe would allow them to think about the rich civilization these Indians had when the pyramids were being built in Egypt.

As the students learned more about these ancient

people, they could learn how to identify animals from their tracks. For this task, students could use Animal Trackers, a program from Sunburst Communications that provides clues from which the students must identify a particular animal. Because this program supports databases for grasslands, desert and wooded areas, it can be used all over the country. Each clue provides information of a different sort – habitat, nesting, food, and footprints. After working with this program for awhile, students will have learned a lot about native American animals, as well as honing their higher order thinking skills. This activity provides an opportunity for science to become integrated with social studies.

As the year proceeds, the students might see a new animal through Indian eyes – the strange creatures with two heads and four legs (the Spanish explorers on horseback). At this point some students might want to retain the Indian perspective and others might want to join forces with Portola or Father Junipero Serra as the colonization of California took place.

Later on in the course, the teacher might show the film Dream West, showing the life of Fremont as he explored the West and paved the way for the United States to expand its boundaries. At this point, students could use the Oregon Trail software from MECC to see how well they might fare in their own journey across the country. This program (one of the first to appear on personal computers) is an excellent simulation of a trip across the country in a covered wagon. It not only reflects the tremendous challenge of such a trip, but hones problem solving skills as each player makes life-

or-death decisions regarding food, camping locations, travel in inclement weather, dealing with hostile environments, etc.

Even though I've just mentioned two pieces of software in this class on history, science, math, language arts, and just about everything else, you probably know of many other excellent programs that you can use to help integrate the curriculum in a meaningful way.

The personal computer running simulation programs can be a wonderful tool for healing a broken curriculum. But, at the same time, there are other appropriate ways to use this technology with children.

Taking Chances

Dr. Kathleen Forsythe, a colleague of mine from British Columbia, defines learning as the perception of newness.

The idea is that anytime we learn something new we perceive it as a discovery. As with discoveries in other domains (such as artistic creativity), learning is risky. We are exposed to new paradigms – to new ways of thinking. These new ways may conflict with our habitual view of the subject domain, and this might cause anxiety. This anxiety may, in turn, make continued learning difficult as we feel our pulse quicken and our hands turn sweaty.

I mention this because, as we explore ways that computer technology can support education, it is clear that some "educational" software supports the student's perception of newness and some does not.

Historically I've chosen to devote my energies to open-ended software that allowed students to explore a subject domain with a great amount of freedom. This has put me at loggerheads with those who feel that computers should be used for drill and practice.

Is there a common ground?

How do we learn?
According to the educational philosopher and Hewlett Packard Vice President Chuck House, learning takes place in four stages:

Stage 1: We don't know that we don't know.
Stage 2: We know that we don't know.
Stage 3: We know that we know.
Stage 4: We don't know that we know.

To illustrate this model, most five-year old children don't know that they don't know integral calculus. By the time these students get to high school, some of them may move to the second stage – they will know that they don't know calculus. A few of these students will then move to the third stage – typically by taking a course in the subject – and they will then know that they know calculus. Finally, after working with this branch of mathematics for a long time, some of these students will become so proficient in this area that their knowledge becomes automatic – they won't "know" that they know the subject.

Much of the conflict between those who endorse using computers as drill tools and those who prefer more open-ended applications are, in fact, just differences of opinion as to whether the computer should be used to move from stage 3 to stage 4 (the domain of practice), or whether it should be used to move the learner from stage 2 to stage 3.

Learning takes place as we move between stages and there is no question that the computer can be an effective tool in the two learning stages we have described. Still, if we look at the ways computers are being used in many classrooms, a great amount of time is being devoted to the drill activity at the expense of discovery learning.

The teacher's role

It is easy to speculate as to why this is the case. First, in contrast to open-ended applications such as LCSI's LogoWriter, drill activities require very little teacher support. The child is placed in front of the computer with a program, and then is left alone to complete the practice in isolation from the rest of the class.

Some computer labs that I've seen look like a page from Orwell's 1984 as thirty or more students sit silently in front of machines where they are being moved, step by step, through activities in which the computer programs the learner. The looks on the faces of these students are generally devoid of expression – much like the zombie stare they acquire in front of a television set.

The result is a student who knows that Springfield is the capitol of Illinois, but who has no idea why the capitol was located there, and, worse yet, has no inclination to even ask the question. To such programs, the student's mind is a vessel to be filled. Still, because many standardized tests look for exactly the kinds of information these programs help students learn, software manufacturers proudly point to the "benefits" of their packages in terms of increased test scores.

If this is the only kind of computing environment that students encounter, their creativity and natural curiosity about the world will atrophy and we will have created a nation of automata.

The times they are a changin'
Our national obsession with fact acquisition has generated some problems. In the area of language arts for example, I've seen students who know the difference between adverbs and adjectives, but who are incapable of writing a coherent sentence. Other students who may know how to write have a horrible time writing a story of their own creation – they seem bereft of ideas.

While it is wrong to lay the blame for this at technology's doorstep, there is little question that increased use of computers as drill machines can easily lead us even further down this path. Ideas, ideas everywhere, but nary a thought to think!

Fortunately, some states have seen the pendulum swing too far, and are working to find a healthy equilibrium point. California, for example, has totally revamped its math, science, social studies and language arts curricula. In language arts, for example, students are moving from worksheets to literature – from multiple choice questions to essays. They are learning that, to write, one must first have an idea to express. How we ever lost sight of these fundamental ideas is beyond me, but I'm happy to see the direction in which the pendulum is now moving.

New software for old ideas
If, in fact, we are changing our educational system in some fairly basic ways, we need to explore how we can best use technology to help students become actively interested and largely self-directed learners. Much of the current multi-media hoopla suggests that anyone

with less than a Mac II at their fingertips belongs to the technological backwater. That, of course, is simply not true. The challenges facing educational computing are not technological. They are challenges of the mind.

The new lever

Archimedes is reputed to have said, give me a lever and a place to put the fulcrum and I can move the world.

The computer and its assorted attachments are a phenomenal educational lever. The insight and infectious love of learning provided by the educator is the fulcrum. If the teacher has sufficient vision, any computer can be used in ways that support true educational discovery. If, on the other hand, this vision is lacking, the computer is likely to become nothing more than a desk ornament.

The funny part about this is that the hardest step to educational reform seems to be the part that costs nothing – vision.

You could place an Apple IIGS with the video overlay card, a CD-ROM player and a video disk on the desk of each child in the classroom, but without the vision of an inspired educator, nothing of value would happen.

Technology and the School of the Future

Print-based education is left-to-right and top-to-bottom in its orientation. This structure of books has rippled through the whole of education to have its impact on both the educational delivery system and on the physical environment in which education takes place. In the early days of formal education, before movable type, lecturers would recite classic works that the students would then transcribe in order to build their own libraries. This task is well-suited for lecture halls in which numerous students face the lecturer at the lectern.

Once books became generally available, the role of the lecturer changed to that of an interpreter of the subject matter. The idea of the teacher as content expert remained and classrooms continued to be designed so all eyes were directed to the front of the room. As long as we perceived the mind as a vessel to be filled rather than as a fire to be kindled, this structure served us well.

Most modern classrooms in this country continue to perpetuate a physical structure that dates, quite literally, to the days before the Renaissance. Nowhere is this more evident than in high school and college classrooms where, in many cases, the seats are even bolted to the floor.

However, in these same buildings, we can see some educators who are adept at kindling fires – teachers whose students are motivated to excel in ways that move them far beyond the skill levels of their instructors. These are the athletic coaches. Their educational environments are designed for the expressed purpose of helping each student to be his/her best in the area of study. A scan of your local sports pages shows how effective these environments can be.

Now that educational computing has clearly moved beyond the fad stage, we need to think about the physical environment in which these computers exist. Computer applications such as Geometry from Brøderbund or MECC's World Geograph are not replicas of the left-to-right top-to-bottom paradigm of print. Instead they, like many other fine programs, allow freedom of exploration in pathways of the user's own construction. This same multi-path ability is found in video disks and is, in fact, a hallmark of most of the educational technology developed in the past 20 years.

But what does it mean to bring a non-linear medium into a rigid classroom which, by its very design, was created for single focal point teaching through a linear sequential process? At best, computers appear here as awkward adjuncts to an iron-age curriculum.

We each have a desire for knowledge, yet we each have our own learning styles, dominant intelligences and unique outlook on life. Educational computing has opened Pandora's box and education will never be the same.

Even so, thousands of teachers insist that their roles

don't need to be examined. They are comfortable with the smell of old oak desks and book pages and chalk dust, and cannot see that their world has not only failed to lead us into the future, it hasn't even kept up with the past. On the other hand, a growing number of educators are exploring teaching methods that honor the whole learner – cooperative learning, teaching to the multiple intelligences and so on. Their classrooms may not be as orderly but their students are fully engaged in the learning process. Computers are comfortable tools in these non-linear environments.

The role of the teacher in these environments ranges from expert to coach to cheerleader, with a smooth transition among these roles. In an appropriately equipped environment students can be provided with an overview and context for the topic of instruction and can then explore the topic largely on their own. For example, history students with access to the Visual Encyclopedia of the Twentieth Century video disks can create their own news reports of historical events in which film clips are interspersed with live interviews of students playing the part of historical figures.

As these changes become more commonplace in our schools we need to think about redesigning our physical plant. For example, any school being built today without provisions for ceiling mounted video projectors in each room is already out of date.

What would an appropriate classroom contain? First the seating arrangement should be flexible. For some tasks students should be able to sit in one large circle. For others they should be able to sit around tables with four to eight students per cluster. A "quiet corner" with comfortable chairs or large pillows would be perfect for those who want to read without being disturbed.

As for technology, a wall-mounted A/V console should accept a variety of media – videotape, videodisk, audio cassettes, digital audio tape and compact disks at the very least. If the cost of this seems high, notice how much of this equipment you probably already have in your home. The audio programming should be directed to a quadraphonic speaker system at the corners of the room. For non-rectangular rooms, other speaker arrangements might be better.

One entire wall of the classroom should be devoted to a rear projection screen behind which lies a video projector capable of creating wall-sized images. The image sources can be controlled from the teacher's workstation. Video overlay cards such as the one provided by Apple will allow the blending and overlay of multiple sources so, for example, student's can overlay rectangles on classic works of art to see how often the Golden Section (1.61801:1) appears.

The students' workspace should provide room for their own notebook computers. This computer would run for weeks on penlight cells and would use a RAM disk to eliminate moving parts. Its display should support both text and high-resolution graphics (monochrome is OK) and the school-based peripherals will give it access to file servers, printers, full screen monitors, disk drives, etc.

The instructional environment of the future should provide a non-linear multi-sensory interface to the natural learning styles of our students.

The issues are not purely technological, they are issues of control. Are you afraid to let your students loose with knowledge? Many in education seem to have adopted the motto, "Don't rock the boat." I suggest that, like the gifted teacher, Keating, in the film Dead Poet's Society, our motto should become "Carpe diem" – "Seize the day!"

Microworlds and Macroworlds

The personal computer is a marvelous tool for exploring conceptual space. It affords unique opportunities to examine microworlds of ones own construction. Furthermore there is almost no limit to the worlds that can be explored.

For example, you could construct a computer world in which gravitational attraction didn't exist, or one for which gravitational attraction dropped with a force proportional to the cube, rather than the square, of the separation between bodies. It is clear that, with microworlds created on the modest computer sitting on your desk, if you can dream it you can do it.

However, as exciting as it is to explore these computational universes of our own creation, I think there is a danger in relying too much on this medium of exploration. For one thing, computational microworlds suffer from a pitfall of science education in general. The pitfall is that, in order to make computations possible, certain simplifying assumptions are made that exchange computability for accuracy.

To see a simple example of this, suppose you were to model the trajectory of a bowling ball that has been pushed off the top of a tall building. A computational model based on the laws of motion would trace a parabolic arc as the ball fell to earth. If you were to actually conduct the experiment, you'd find that the real trajectory was close, but not precisely the same as the one you'd calculated. Furthermore, you'd find, with repeated experiments, that the ball would most likely not fall on the same spot twice, but land at slightly different locations for each experiment.

This gap between the computer simulation and the real world of physics has several causes. First, the computer model might not have allowed for wind resistance. It most likely would not have compensated for various gusts of wind to which the ball was exposed on its trajectory. The model might even have assumed that the ground was flat.

While such simplifying assumptions make calculations tractable, and help us to see the major structure of physical phenomena, they make it easy for us to think that we live in a predictable world, when predictability is the exception, not the rule.

While it is true that a computer model of a falling body will come close to predicting the results of the actual experiment, most dynamic systems are very sensitive to slight perturbations. This means that a slight error in starting assumptions can produce tremendously varied results. This is the case for weather prediction, for example, and we can even model some of this sensitivity with some of the chaotic functions we explore elsewhere (see Chaotic Microworlds in the references).

Bringing the worlds together
The cure for this is to balance theory with actual experiments by creating environments in which computer models (microworlds) interact with reality (the macroworld) in a meaningful way.

Brøderbund and Sunburst Communications have light and heat sensors that can be used to provide physical data to the computer where this data can be displayed and analyzed. These products are a step in the right direction in that they allow us to explore real phenomena, complete with all the "errors" and perturbations that attend any physical experiment. It seems to me, though, that the challenge is not to just use the computer as a data capturing tool, but to use it to allow the interactive exploration of concepts through an integrated blend of computational models and physical experiments.

Meeting of the screens

As an example of what I'm thinking about, imagine the following configuration of equipment: An Apple IIe with the Apple Video Overlay card and the Logo programming language, and a Canon Zap Shot or Sony Mavica video still camera. The computer holds the microworlds created with Logo, the video still camera holds macroworlds in the form of still full-color images, and these worlds are brought together through the video overlay card. You could spend a day in the woods photographing plants with the camera (in effect, creating your own video disks). By later connecting the camera's video output to the video overlay card, you could then see your color images on the computer screen, and could then have the computer add its own graphics to your photographs through programs created in Logo.

As a starting activity, you might want to see whether the golden rectangle (a rectangle with side ratios of 1.618:1) appears in any of the objects you photographed.

With a few simple commands, you could draw a rectangle of this proportion around a photograph of a pine cone to see if it fits. Later on, you might want to try replicating the pattern of a fern bract using a recursive pattern in which the overall shape of the bract is self-similar to the shape of an individual leaf. By having a photo of the plant displayed underneath your computer generated image, any similarities and differences will be very easy to see.

Such explorations are not limited to the natural sciences. The golden rectangle experiment works beautifully with photographs of classical architecture and other works of art. The domain for the integration of macro and microworlds is boundless.

Macroworlds in the classroom
At another level, this integration of two worlds through technology may be a metaphor for a transformation in education. Far too many of our classrooms operate as microworlds isolated from the real world. Confined to rooms without telephones, satellite down-link videos from around the world, and other communication advances that have turned our huge planet into a global village, our 19th century classrooms perpetuate a model of education that has lost touch with reality.

Just as physics books present inaccurate models in exchange for computability, we are continuing to support an educational system that perpetuates models that are ignorant of both technological advances and the fact that our world is growing increasingly complex.

Simplifying assumptions have their place to the extent that they allow us to understand certain basic principles, but they become dangerous when they are accepted as being true.

I remember hearing from a parent whose child was asked if a ball rolled off the edge of a table would fall to the ground in the same time as a ball dropped straight down from the same height. The child said no, and the teacher marked the answer wrong. The parent protested, pointing out that the earth is curved. This meant that the dropped ball would land before the one that rolled horizontally off the table. The teacher held fast, and the argument grew as the parent finally accused the teacher of belonging to the Flat Earth Society.

I tell this story because we in education must be careful to acknowledge the wonderfully complex world outside the classroom walls – a world of imperfections, yes, but a world without limits – a world in which our children will invent both their and our future.

The Role of Technology in Teaching to the Whole Child

Multiple Intelligences in the Classroom

Many of today's classrooms are set up to teach to children as though they were linguistic, logical-mathematical learners. Children whose dominant learning styles fall outside these domains are often frustrated. Their dominant styles reveal themselves through humming, doodling, fidgeting, talking, or behaving in ways that are disruptive to the dominant model of the classroom. In extreme cases, these children become identified as "learning disabled" because they seem incapable of learning subjects the way they are generally taught.

Research at Harvard has shown that each of us has components of seven distinct intelligences, any of which can be our dominant intelligence. An educational system that teaches to all of these intelligences honors the thinking styles of each individual and can help retain the natural joy of learning.

The challenge comes from trying to teach to the whole mind of all learners when there is only one teacher in a room with 30 or more students. In what follows we will explore ways that technology – specifically the classroom computer – can be used to allow each student to learn virtually any subject through his/her dominant intelligence while increasing the facility of the other intelligences as well.

We have yet to construct a thorough plan for integrating technology at all grades and in all subject areas, yet there is much that we can do to honor the dominant intelligences of students. The simple act of using a computer program as a bridge from the student's dominant mode to the natural mode of the subject can do much to help students feel better about themselves and their capabilities.

Each of us involved with education wants to help children be their best – to become all they can be. Historically, our interest in educational computing was born out of a belief that this technology would help children become better able to grasp concepts. One of the prime attractors of educational computing in the late 1970's was the promise that it would simplify the individualization of education by allowing each learner to proceed at his or her own rate. This feature, coupled with the computer's ability to provide auditory and visual rewards, made the computer into an updated version of the behaviorist tools developed by B. F. Skinner.

While educational computing grew in popularity, the behaviorist view, reflected in a plethora of drill software, became only one of numerous paths down which this technology was led. The opposite extreme from the behaviorist view was found in the Piagetian approach to education embodied in Logo. Those few educators able to keep up with both pedagogy and technology were able to pick and choose from a wide spectrum of computer-based activities that benefited their students.

But, by in large, most educators found the waters of educational computing so muddied that they dared not get their toes wet.

Letting computers bloom...

The recent surge of interest in thinking skills development has resulted in a marriage between Bloom's taxonomy of thinking and software for personal computers. As commonly expressed, Professor Bloom's taxonomy consists of the following six thinking skills:

1   Knowledge
2   Comprehension
3   Application
4   Analysis
5   Synthesis
6   Evaluation

Each of these six skills is important and yet, until recently, contemporary education has not emphasized the "higher-order" skills of analysis, synthesis and evaluation. In an effort to apply technology to remedy this perceived deficiency, many software developers worked hard to create programs that addressed the development of higher-order thinking across the curriculum. While many of the drill-based programs are directed toward the development of the lower-order skills, the catalogs of publishers like The Learning Company and Sunburst Communications (to name just two) are filled with programs that help students learn how to analyze complex situations, to create solutions from a synthesis of existing parts, and to articulate the thinking processes that led them to a solution.

A different approach
While this formal attempt to correlate software with thinking skills is laudatory, it is incomplete. While acknowledging the need to develop all thinking skills in all children, it ignores the potential of the personal computer to truly individualize instruction.

Traditionally, computer-based individualization assumed that students differed in their speed of learning, not in their intrinsic learning styles. We are now on the threshold of a new understanding that will allow educational computing to reach its potential. The key to unlocking this secret lies within the learner – not the teacher.

Multiple Intelligences
Many years ago a study on IQ test scores was conducted to see what correlation, if any, could be found between these scores and performance. While it was found that there was a high level of correlation between IQ scores and academic performance, there was no correlation between these scores and performance outside the classroom. In other words, there are as many geniuses on skid row as there are in corporate board rooms.

This observation intrigued Professor Howard Gardner at Harvard who launched into a detailed study of intelligence by looking at the performance of prodigies, idiots savant and others with special gifts. His work was published in the book, *Frames of Mind*. As a result of his study he concluded that each of us has at least seven intelligences including:

- Linguistic
- Logical-Mathematical
- Intrapersonal
- Spatial
- Musical
- Bodily-Kinesthetic
- Interpersonal

While each of us may dominate in one of these seven areas, we all have capabilities in the other six.

Research in accelerated learning or "superlearning" techniques has shown that students can learn new subjects at phenomenal rates when provided with the right environment. One of the things that distinguishes a superlearning experience from the traditional classroom is that it teaches to all the intelligences. For example, during a one-week accelerated course in French conducted by the Barzak Learning Institute we listened, wrote, played games, worked by ourselves, drew pictures, sang songs, danced and talked with each other. Furthermore, these activities were integrated into a cohesive whole. While the principles of superlearning were developed independently of Professor Gardner's work, the pieces of the puzzle all fit together quite nicely.

The atmosphere in today's classroom is often quite

different. Our tendency is to teach to the linguistic, logical-mathematical, and intrapersonal learner and to virtually ignore the other intelligences. This tendency has two negative consequences. First, it ignores the needs of the child whose dominant intelligence is not one of these three. Second, it misses the chance to validate and develop the other intelligences in all the children in the room. Time and time again we have found that, the more ways a subject is presented, the better that subject is learned and remembered.

The Harvard work is a floodlight that illuminates a new path for education – one that can do much to help children retain their natural love for learning.

Multiple Intelligences and Computers

It is logical to ask at this point just how a classroom teacher is supposed to tailor a curriculum to the different intelligences. Is the bodily-kinesthetic child supposed to practice his spelling words by writing them on the school wall with a squirt gun? (Not a bad idea, by the way.) Many marvelous ideas get lost in implementation because they are too time consuming or because they pull educators in new directions too fast.

Fortunately, computer technology is tailor-made to allow education to reach the dominant intelligence of each child.

The reason for tying computer activities to the intelligences is very simple: From the beginning of the personal computer revolution we have been told that this technology would allow the individualization of instruction. For many people that meant nothing more than allowing instruction to be self-paced. Now, with this powerful theory to guide us, we can bring that dream into sharp focus. First, we can explore the match between the software we already have and the dominant intelligences of our children. Second, we can highlight areas for which new software needs to be created and, best of all, we can develop specific sets of criteria by which such software can be judged. To my mind, this is the focus that has been missing in educational computing.

Computers: 3 R's for the 2 L's

We will next explore programs appropriate for those with dominant linguistic and logical-mathematical intelligences. In thinking about this topic it is important to keep two thoughts in mind. First, every one of us has all seven intelligences to varying degrees – we each have skills in the linguistic, logical-mathematical, spatial, musical, bodily-kinesthetic, intrapersonal and interpersonal domains. Second, the purpose of exploring computer software that corresponds to these domains is not just to develop skills in these areas, but more importantly, to use native skills in these areas to explore topics that might be more naturally explored through one of the other intelligences.

Obviously, it would be impossible to provide a comprehensive list of software in even one of these seven areas. First, as we discussed above, within any subject area and dominant intelligence type there are at least six thinking skills that can be developed with software. At the barest minimum we would have to list 42 programs (six thinking skills and seven intelligences) for each subject (fourth-grade social studies, for example.) Instead of tackling this massive task, we will take one or two examples of computer-based activities in each of the seven intelligences and show how they can be applied in certain subject areas where the connection may not be obvious. Hopefully, this exercise will allow you to look at your own software library in a new light. It will allow you to tailor both primary and supplemental instruction to the dominant intelligence type of each child in your classroom.

Getting your word's worth

Because language arts are such a pivotal part of today's curriculum, the obvious match between the highly linguistic student and this subject area results in an obvious list of software suitable for these students. At the top of the list are word processors.

We must be careful, though, when choosing word processors for the classroom. The child who wants to write should be able to write with as few inhibitions as possible. My personal tendency is to lean towards the simpler programs that have the good sense to stay out of the user's way. The writer should be able to boot the disk and start writing. Even Appleworks – one of the better programs in my view – engages the user in irrelevant dialogue prior to starting a document.

There are several word processors designed for the very young writer. These products provide a moderately consistent user interface as the user progresses from level to level. For example, the

Muppet Slate word processor from Sunburst can be used with the Muppet Learning Keys or the Apple II keyboard. It was designed with the K-2 student in mind and it allows simple graphics to be incorporated with text. In other words, a picture of an elephant can be inserted in a line of text instead of having to write the word "elephant".

The rebus-like quality of this product is intriguing. All letter shapes in our language started out as pictures of things. Many educators (especially those associated with the Waldorf schools) believe that children should be introduced to written language through pictures.

For those who don't want pictures with their text, Sunburst's Magic Slate II is available in three versions, providing 20-, 40- and 80- columns of text on the screen. The 20 column version is geared to the child through grade 3, while the other versions can be used by older students. The 80-column product provides more sophisticated formatting tools than the others, making it appropriate for the high-school and college audience.

The challenge of computer use for the linguistic learner has never been software, it has been access. Writing is a time-consuming process. If the student's only access to computers is for 15 minutes a week in a computer lab, a word processor is probably the worst program to let these students see. It produces what my IBM friend, Harvey Long, calls an "anti-Pavlovian" response – "If you haven't got the food, don't ring my bell!"

W_eel of Fo_tune
Until we have enough computers to allow unlimited access to word processing, we should explore other programs to support the linguistic learner. Hangman-like games in which the user guesses letters to complete a word have the advantage that they can be used effectively in a computer-lab setting. My own preference is for games that involve complete phrases rather than isolated words, such as M_ss_ng L_nks from Sunburst. The player can often choose a missing letter based on the overall structure of the sentence and his or her knowledge of the kinds of words one is likely to find in certain places. To the extent that there is a logic to the structure of language, the player can develop his or her logical-mathematical intelligence through a linguistic activity.

Fertile Fields
It is this type of cross-fertilization across the intelligence boundaries that educators should be looking for when choosing software. For example, text-based adventure games like those found in Scholastic's Microzine have the ability to help the linguistic learner develop spatial reasoning skills as he or she navigates through mazes. The Learning Company's Reader Rabbit blends the linguistic and spatial domains to improve reading skills.

I Compute Therefore I Am
As with the linguistic domain, the world of the logical-mathematical thinker is richly supported in most classrooms. The whole basis for digital computers is built on logic and symbol manipulation. As a result, there are hundreds of excellent computer programs

designed to develop skills in this area. Even so, we should be cautious in prescribing software for students who are masters of this domain.

For example, let's look at two popular programs associated with the development of logical thinking skills, both designed by the same person, Dr. Thomas O'Brien from the Teacher's Center Project at Southern Illinois University at Edwardsville. The two titles are King's Rule and Safari Search (both published by Sunburst.) While both of these programs are designed to develop logical-mathematical thought, they perform this task in two completely different ways.

In King's Rule the student is provided with a set of numbers that fit a rule. For example: 2, 6, 2 and 1, 8, 1 might fit a rule. By experimenting with other sets of numbers the user is told whether they fit or not. For example, 0, 10, 0 does fit and 3, 5, 3 does not. The user (when ready) can ask to be tested. The computer might ask if 2, 2, 6 fits the rule (it does). Through experimentation the user can decide that the rule is that the sum of the numbers is 10. The program never explicitly confirms this, however. King's Rule is an example of a logical-mathematical program designed for the logical-mathematical thinker.

In Safari Search, the user is provided with a checker board-like square on which a character is hiding. At each level of the game the user is provided with various clues to help lead the player to the hidden creature. If the player picks a square close to the square containing the creature, the word HOT or WARM may appear to indicate that the goal is connected to the chosen square by an edge or a corner, respectively. By picking a few squares and looking at the messages, the player can then decide with certainty where the creature is hidden. This program is an example of a logical-mathematical program designed for the spatial thinker.

Both programs help to develop similar skills, but they reach the learner through different intelligences.

The Art of Mathematics
A challenge to today's computer-using educator is to identify computer-based activities that allow the logical-mathematical learner to explore subjects and learning modes that are remote from this area. While this task may be hard, it isn't impossible.

To provide one small example, let's look at a digitized copy of Rafael's Madonna of the Table (shown above.)

This exquisite painting hangs in the Pitti Palace in Florence. During a tour of the gallery I was told that, if you were to draw a fixed-pitch spiral starting at the infant's elbow, it would go through the mother's elbow, through the infant's eyes, through her eyes, and through the eyes of the third person. Obviously, this couldn't be tested in the gallery. But, by making a digitized copy of a slide of this picture, one can test this hypothesis with the computer.

When the correct spiral is drawn by the computer, you can see that the tour guide was right!

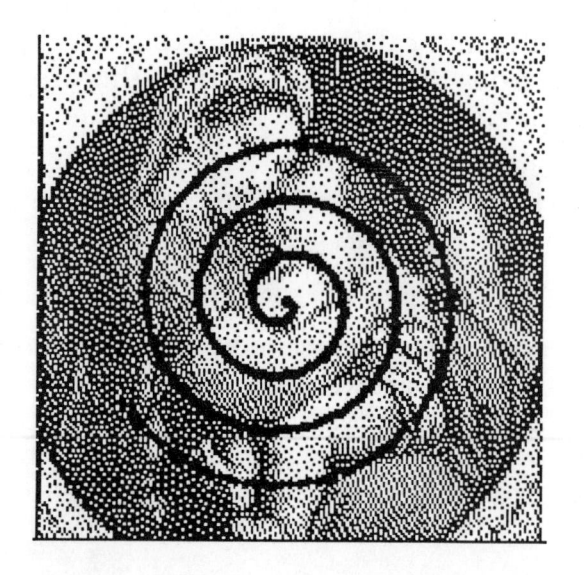

The point of this exercise is very simple. It allows the mathematical-logical thinker to look at art in a new way – to become sensitive to underlying pattern and structural form that can be found in many of the great works hanging in galleries throughout the world. This brief computer activity is designed to help open the door to spatial thinking for the person whose dominant mode is logical- mathematical.

Computers in Space and Music

Our topics in this section are of special importance since these intelligences are not usually supported in today's classrooms. Support for painting and music, for example, is high in the primary years, but falls off sharply as children reach higher grades. Worse yet, the integration of these areas into the curriculum is virtually non-existent.

On the surface one may not see this as causing problems, but it does. Research at the California State University in Chico has suggested that one of the reasons boys tends to score better on standardized math tests than girls is because boys use fast "spatial" reasoning to solve problems while girls tend to use slower "linguistic" methods. Examinations given without time constraints produce equivalent scores for both sexes, but differences show up as soon as the questions must be answered in a hurry.

This work strongly suggests that we need to develop the spatial reasoning ability of all children – especially girls.

If the incorporation of the musical domain into the curriculum seems harder to justify, this is probably because the topic is virtually unexplored. To enter most classrooms today one would think that music had never been invented. And yet, throughout the planet, I know of no culture without music. There is no question in my mind that the power of music and its relevance to subjects as diverse as history and mathematics suggests that we do more in the classroom in this area. Fortunately, for the development of both the spatial and musical intelligences, computer tools are abundant.

Isn't that spatial!

One of the easiest ways to explore spatial reasoning with students of any age is through the use of Logo's "turtle graphics". The Logo programming language is equipped with a rich collection of graphics tools that allow students to create geometric shapes at any location or orientation on the screen. With this language a child can make discoveries on his/her own. By experimenting with the creation of complex shapes that can be drawn in mirror reflection from each other, students can reinforce the kind of spatial reasoning that is required to perform well on standardized tests.

Several years ago my wife had a student who appeared to be incapable of distinguishing a square from a pentagon when both figures were drawn on the board. After working with Logo for a short period of time, this child worked through his perceptual blocks and was able to generate, recognize and properly identify a tremendous variety of polygons. I believe that, by building shapes line by line, children introduced to geometry through Logo develop "insights" that assist in the reinforcement and development of their spatial intelligence.

Interactive maps

The student in social studies who just can't make sense

from a table of numbers can often "see" connections when this same information is presented graphically. One product that beautifully meets this need is World GeoGraph for the Apple IIGS. This product, produced by the Minnesota Educational Computing Corporation, is a geographical database that supports information on 177 nations around the world. This information can be displayed in the form of graphs or colored maps.

By looking at information shown as different colors on the maps, students can make observations regarding trends that would be far harder to grasp if they were presented as tables of numbers. The user can zoom in on a region of interest, observe patterns of similarities and differences among nations, observing correlations among economic and cultural data, etc.

Through this program, students can add or edit database categories and can start to develop a feel for the relationships – both spatial and sociopolitical – among the many nations on our planet.

A similar product, PC Globe, provides much of the same capability on MS-DOS-based computers.

Other spaces
The ability of personal computers to plot complex equations allows math students to develop a concrete feeling for abstract mathematical concepts. The math courses I took in college used trivially simple functions to illustrate concepts because they were easy to plot by hand. Today's students have a potential advantage over those of my generation because of the graphics capability of their computers.

Sensei's Geometry program (available from Brøderbund for both the Macintosh and Apple IIGS) is a stellar example of what can be done in this area. Designed to support a complete course in Euclidian geometry, this program allows students to explore geometrical concepts ranging from congruence to complex theorems with the aid of animated graphics that illustrate the consequences of various constraints or assumptions on various classes of geometric shapes. Sensei's other products – Physics and Calculus – bring this excellent approach to other subject domains.

Students with nothing but the built-in Applesoft BASIC interpreter can create excellent plotting programs of their own.

Music
To muse is to ponder or think about something – a solid educational concept. And yet the related word, music, seems to have lost its place in contemporary education. Music is at the heart of human existence. The overwhelming popularity of music can be verified by counting the number of music stations as you tune your radio across the dial.

MIDI to the Max
No one has ever claimed that the unadorned personal computer is an interesting music machine. The sound generation capabilities of this computer are limited to puny peeps generated through a tiny loudspeaker. The Apple IIGS, on the other hand, has sound generation capabilities that rival many commercial synthesizers.

Even so, the real musical power of these computers (including the GS) comes less from their own capabilities than from their ability to control external synthesizers through a MIDI interface. Inexpensive MIDI interfaces can be obtained from several sources including Passport Designs and Apple. Because many consumer level and all studio grade synthesizers have MIDI interfaces, your computer can control an amazing array of instruments ranging from percussion ensembles to complete orchestras.

Thus far, music software for personal computers has fallen into two general classes: sequencers and transcription systems. A sequencer can be thought of as a multi-track recorder that records all the keystrokes and other information sent by a synthesizer. This information can be edited and sent back through the synthesizer to allow the piece to be replayed in another key or even on another instrument. Transcription programs allow musical scores to be created and printed out. Some of these programs capture music as it is played on the keyboard and then place these notes on the score for further editing. Pyware's Music Writer for the Apple IIGS and Activision's Music Studio for the Apple II are two popular programs that bridge the gap between the computer and synthesizer.

What is missing is a hook that allows any program to send MIDI-based melodies to external synthesizers as an alternative to the internal beeps and clicks generated by the computer itself. Now that MIDI synthesizers are available for under $200 we should at least expect our programs to offer us more choices in this area.

CD's and computers
CD-quality audio is available under computer control through use of CD-ROM technology. This area is so intriguing that we devote the next chapter to it.

Music in the classroom?
For certain learners, music can be the gateway to knowledge. The mood of a piece of music might communicate, clearer than words, the feeling of an era being studied in history. The exploration of rhythm can help some students understand fractions. The exploration of the sounds of an organ pipe can lead to an understanding of vibrational modes in physics.

If you are still unconvinced, ask yourself this question: What caused the great scientist Kepler to think of the motions of planets in musical terms? Astronomy students could program a synthesizer to play Kepler's "music of the spheres" and explore history, science, math and music all at once.

Learners who are unable to use piano keyboards can still explore music on the computer through the use of the Vocalizer 1000 from Breakaway Systems. This versatile instrument works by humming into the mouthpiece. The pitch of your voice is then converted to the nearest note and is replayed through the MIDI port or through a built-in synthesizer.

Breakthroughs in computer-based music tools are taking place faster than we can accommodate them. Of all the intelligences we will explore, the musical is the most ignored, and yet it is also the most universal.

Let's get physical
People who display a highly developed bodily-kinesthetic intelligence are good at motor activities such as sports and dancing. They have a well-developed sense of their body and how it moves in relation to the surrounding world.

At first glance it might seem that computer technology is too limiting to offer much to people for whom this is their dominant mode. The bodily-kinesthetic child often has a hard time in a traditional classroom. He or she finds it hard to sit in one place for an extended period of time. If this child is moved from the desk to the computer, one might expect fidgeting to set in pretty quickly.

For this reason, it is appealing to think of computer activities that involve body movement. Two obvious applications that come to mind are Lego Logo and Brøderbund's Science Toolkit. Both of these computer activities involve external manipulatives that are connected to the computer in such a way that the computer can act as a controller or as a receiver for experiments that the student has constructed with his or her own hands.

The Lego Logo materials consist of a set of Lego blocks with wheels and gears and motors that can be controlled by commands given from a special version of the Logo programming language. Students are free to build their own robots or other mechanical devices which can then be operated under the control of student-generated computer programs.

Tools like the Science Toolkit or Sunburst's Exploring Science materials operate a bit differently. Instead of using the computer to control an external device, the computer becomes a tool to receive data from external temperature, light or motion probes. This data can then be analyzed and displayed in graphical form on the display screen. Because the student has the task of physically assembling an experiment and installing the computer probes, this concrete activity supports the needs of the bodily- kinesthetic learner.

Lego Logo provides a bridge from the bodily-kinesthetic to the spatial domain. The Science Toolkit provides a bridge from the bodily-kinesthetic to the Logical-Mathematical domain.

Personally speaking

The student with a highly developed intrapersonal intelligence has a good sense of self and is often highly motivated to work things out for him or herself. Because the computer supports this one-on-one style of operation very easily, we should not be surprised to find that the intrapersonal learner gravitates toward the creation of computer programs or the playing of complex games.

The bulk of educational computer software seems to be geared to the "lone wolf" computer user, so it is easy to find computer tools that support the intrapersonal learner. By allowing these children to create their own databases or programs for the exploration of specific topics, you can easily bring these children into contact with other intelligence domains.

Logo programming, for example, can develop skills in the spatial and logical-mathematical domains. Database construction can form a bridge to the interpersonal domain as the student describes the database to others, and works with others to extend the database on any subject of interest to the class.

The greatest challenge for this learner is computer access. If the classroom only has one computer, it is hard to find the kind of unrestricted time that the intrapersonal learner needs to explore topics on his or her own.

Social computing

The development of software geared to the needs of the interpersonal learner is fairly recent. Among the titles that seem to fit this need, Decisions, Decisions by Tom Snyder Publications is a good example. In this program, each user takes the part of someone running for elected office. During the course of the campaign, each participant has to make decisions and tradeoffs that often present conflicts between the integrity of the campaign and the desire to capture as many votes as possible. The activity supports several computer-based "advisors" who can be asked for help at various stages of the campaign. When several students are using the program at the same time, the opportunity exists for the campaign to continue in the classroom, not just on the computer.

As with other programs from Tom Snyder, Decisions, Decisions is geared to the needs of the interpersonal learner while making optimal use of one computer in a classroom.

Other applications of interest to the interpersonal child include access to bulletin board services and correspondence with electronic "pen pals." As an example of how powerful this environment can be, Apple's research project, Apple Global Education, has allowed students in numerous countries to communicate with each other through their computers. Student generated projects have spanned a wide range of subjects and interests. For example, one student in San Jose, California sent his Spanish homework to a student in Spain for review. Students have collected local legends, jump rope chants, recipes and information on many other topics and then shared this information with colleagues around the world. Projects like this show the tremendous power of interpersonal computing as students developing and understanding and appreciation for the diverse cultures supported on our fragile planet.

Unfortunately, very few classrooms have telephone lines with modems to allow such communication to take place. Even so, educators can simulate this type of an environment by setting up a computer with a word processor program on which students can enter their own messages to the class. The messages can be printed out at the end of the day before erasing the screen for the next day's messages.

Making sense
In choosing the various intelligences, Professor Gardner was careful to not link them directly with the senses. For example, while we might immediately link spatial intelligence with vision and musical

intelligence with hearing, one can find examples of each of these intelligences operating in the other's domain. The structure of a fugue, for example, may been seen as highly geometric. Alternatively, the sight of a meadow filled with flowers may evoke a mental playing of a favorite piece of music.

His decision to separate the intelligences from the senses was not meant to downplay the role of the senses, for it is through them that we interact with and gain knowledge of the world around us.

The sensory machine

If, as we have suggested, computer software is a bridge to the intelligences, then it is through the hardware that our senses are engaged in meaningful communication across this bridge.

Assuming for a moment that we can assign dominant senses to the intelligences, we can build the following table:

Intelligence	Dominant Sense(s)
Linguistic	Hearing, Vision
Logical-Mathematical	Vision, Mentation
Spatial	Vision
Musical	Hearing
Bodily-Kinesthetic	Touch, Motion
Interpersonal	Hearing, Vision
Intrapersonal	Mentation

This table lists two non-standard senses – mentation (the sense of conscious thought) and motion, our kinesthetic sense. The dominant sensory modes in our table are vision and hearing – modalities that computers have historically addressed well. Through appropriate input devices (and off-line activities) touch is introduced, leaving mentation as the sense to be engaged by the content of the software.

Designing a system

In designing a computer system for learning there are two criteria of major importance. First, the technology needs to be so powerful that it gets out of the user's way. I believe this can be accomplished with an Apple IIe, and certainly with the Apple IIGS as the heart of the system. Macintoshes and other higher-end products make the task even easier. If you are just starting out, you'll find that a new system can provide a phenomenal amount of capability in a single box.

Second, we need to consider the design of two systems – one for use by the teacher from the front of the room, and another to be used by individual students. Because universal access to computers is still a distant dream for most educators, our focus will be on the teacher's machine.

A Computer for the teacher

The educator's workstation should threaten the blackboard. When large writing surfaces are needed, the classroom should have one of the new writing board technologies (such as that made by Fuji Xerox) that automatically reduces the content of the blackboard to 8 1/2" by 11" copies with its built-in copier. Of course, every classroom should have its own reprographic center with a copier, binding equipment, etc. so students can prepare complete documents ranging from one-page memos to their own books.

As for the computer itself, the teacher should have at least an Apple IIGS (or equivalent MS-DOS machine) with 1 megabyte or more of RAM. Both 5.25" and 3.5" disk drives and a CD-ROM drive should be available so that all software can be used with ease. A 20 megabyte hard disk is well worth the investment.

If you are buying a new system, be sure it comes with a built-in CD-ROM drive. Any computer made today without one is a quaint anachronism that has no place in a classroom of the 90's.

The video capabilities of the computer should be enhanced with a video overlay card that allows the computer image to be intermixed with any video source – VCR, videodisk, etc. Panasonic has an inexpensive titling machine that can be used in this fashion, and Apple's Video Overlay Card works with any Apple II or IIGS computer. Other devices of this type are entering the marketplace as more and more people become interested in creating their own video productions. The Commodore Amiga's capabilities in this area are so excellent that many television stations use the Amiga for some of their own video overlay needs.

At first glance this addition might be thought of as a replacement for a second monitor, but in fact it is much more than that. A frozen image of a dividing cell on a video disk can be "drawn on" by the teacher to highlight those cell parts being studied. The combination of internal and external visual images connects the microworlds of the computer to the macroworld of life. Imagine the art/math activity based on the Rafael painting we described with our digitized image replaced by a full color television quality image from a videodisk!

The output of this combined video should be connected to an RGB monitor on the teacher's desk and to a color video projector whose image can be seen by the whole class without requiring that the lights be shut off and the drapes pulled. The Kodak (now Epson) LC-500 projector is about the size of a slide projector and is a hint of what lies ahead in this exciting area of technology. Unlike the earlier liquid crystal displays that sat on top of hot overhead projectors, the LC-500 shows images in full color and has a fast enough response time to show moving images. The slightly larger video projectors from Sharp are less portable but produce brighter, clearer, images.

External video sources at the teacher's fingertips should include a high-quality VCR with freeze frame capability and a laser videodisk player with an RS-232 interface allowing it to be controlled by the computer. Computer controlled VCR's, while feasible, have not made it into the domain of reasonable prices yet.

A sound choice
In the sound domain, the IIGS should have a MIDI

interface connected to a high quality synthesizer. While low-cost MIDI synthesizers are tremendous assets for any classroom, their timbres (instrument sounds) can become grating after awhile. My preference is to look at instruments such as the Kurzweil K1000 because it supports alternative tunings (useful in studying music/physics) and it has a rich collection of wonderful instrument sounds. Alternatively, a good sampling synthesizer (one that allows you to capture a sound of your own, edit it, and assign it to musical notes) is a tool of tremendous value. The Ensoniq EPS or the Casio FZ-1 are two choices here. Be aware that the electronic music field is advancing rapidly, and that last year's hottest synthesizer might be available at a great price! If you already have a MIDI keyboard, you can add more sounds with MIDI sound modules or expansion units. These are complete synthesizers without keyboards, such as the Casio VZ-10M.

A speech synthesizer can be a useful addition to the computer, especially when the audience includes students who are still learning how to read. While high quality speech synthesis is possible in computers like the Apple IIGS, many speech synthesizers produce barely intelligible output. When the computer is being used from the front of the room, it is probably better for the speaking to be done by humans, not machines.

Rounding it out
Of course a printer is essential. If you can live with black and white, a LaserWriter is a good choice. For color you may have to live with a dot-matrix impact printer for awhile longer.

CD-ROM applications are proliferating, making a CD-ROM drive a good investment for your existing computers. We'll discuss the power of this technology in the next chapter.

The student's setup
With the exception of the projection display, the student should have access to the same technology being used by the teacher.

Compromises
The system described above is fairly expensive. For example, an MS-DOS '386 system with built-in CD-ROM, 3 1/2" disk drive, VGA color monitor, 40 megabyte hard disk and 2 megabytes of RAM will run about $2500. Compromises can and will be made by anyone trying to implement these ideas.

Much of what is needed to implement these workstations already exists in many schools, it just hasn't been hooked together. By bringing music, graphics, video, massive libraries and powerful software under the control of one keyboard, one can quickly find that the whole is greater than the sum of its parts. Magic can be created with an Apple IIe, existing VCR's, a $200 synthesizer and a standard monitor. The challenges are not technological – they are challenges of our intention. If we truly want to teach to the whole mind, technology will always support us.

The fact that we now have a matching pedagogical and technological base suggests that we can truly transform education in a way that will preserve the joy of learning that we all had before we entered school. The development of each of us as proactive life-long learners is essential for our survival.

Technology is one tool that exists to serve the needs of those who make the magic happen – you, the teachers.

CD-ROMS and Educational Computing

The educational computing domain has had few exciting announcements since 1984 when the Macintosh redefined the concept of user interfaces for many people. Until very recently, most technology developments have centered on price reduction and incremental improvements in speed, memory capacity, etc. Except for these features, most classroom computers look the same today as they did six years ago. A similar story can be told for educational software. Except for a few blockbuster titles (such as Brøderbund's Carmen Sandiego series and the like) most educational software has only incrementally extended the things were were doing years ago.

Now, however, I think were are being exposed to a technological development so powerful that it has the potential to impact education as much as the personal computer could – and this technology is an inexpensive peripheral for the technology we already have.

I'm talking about the CD-ROM.

For those of you unfamiliar with the technology, let's look first at the outstanding success of the compact audio disk. This technology has been the fastest growing consumer technology for the past few years, and it will soon render the phonograph obsolete. Each compact disk can hold up to 70 minutes or so of exceptionally high quality audio programming on a 5 inch plastic disk whose surface is read by a laser beam. The absence of any physical contact with the playing surface makes these disks playable forever, and they are even moderately insensitive to fingerprints and other physical damage. Audio programming is stored on these disks in digital form, and this information is then reconstructed as audio signals in the CD player.

Because the recording format is digital, these disks can be used to hold computer programs and data. The amount of information that can be stored on one disk staggers the imagination. I have one disk in my collection that has 640 million bytes of Macintosh software on it. To grasp how much this is, each standard Mac disk holds about 800 thousand byes of data. Imagine a stack of 800 Macintosh disks (a stack over 8 feet tall). This is what would be required to save the data that can be put on one 5 inch CD-ROM that can be manufactured (in volume) for about $2 apiece.

The downside...
Unlike magnetic disks, CD-ROMs are "read-only" - you can't add information to them (yet). As software distribution vehicles, they are unsurpassed, but you'll still need magnetic disks to hold your own data and programs.

The reason I'm excited about this technology for education is two-fold: When you have over 640 megabytes at your fingertips, personal computing undergoes a qualitative change – it doesn't feel the same anymore. One disk from World Library (The Library of the Future disk) contains 450 literary, historical, cultural and religious works on a single disk. Titles include the Confessions of St. Augustine, Chaucer's Canterbury Tales, the works of Arthur Conan Doyle, John Milton, Aristotle, Epictetus, Shakespeare, Whitman and numerous others. Just looking at a directory on a disk this huge is cause for awe, and it almost has to be experienced to be believed. If this isn't enough, the compression method used by World Library allows an additional 600 volumes to be stored on the same disk, bringing over 1000 classic works to the fingertips of a student – all on one CD-ROM disk that can be put in a coat pocket.

In addition to holding computer readable information, the same disk can contain the high quality audio found on traditional CD's, along with television quality video segments and a host of other signals. In other words, the CD-ROM has the potential to incorporate complete multi-media presentations in one delivery medium.

Who needs it?
640 megabytes is almost an unthinkably large amount of memory. What kind of application could possibly take advantage of this capability? One that comes to mind is a CD-ROM version of the desk encyclopedia. Comptons has placed their entire encyclopedia on this medium, with a twist. In addition to the text entries associated with each item, the disk contains picture and sound files. An exploration of "Mozart", for example, provides a traditional entry on his life, a color picture for the computer screen, and a compressed sound file with the opening strains of Eine Kleine Nachtmusik.

Other types of reference books and massive databases

are straightforward choices for this medium, but they are by no means the only applications that come to mind.

Dylan's disk...

Because the CD-ROM disk drive (which traditionally uses an SCSI port and costs as little as $500) can play your audio disks as well as communicate with the computer, users of HyperCard and other software that can communicate with these devices can create applications built entirely around the audio CD's you may already have at home.

A friend of mine in British Columbia, Gerri Sinclair, showed me a project of hers that illustrates the power of this medium. She took a CD recording of Dylan Thomas reading Fern Hill (one of his most beautiful poems) and painstakingly indexed each word of the poem by its location on the disk. Because the CD-ROM drive can select any time location on the disk to an accuracy of 1/75 of a second, she had total control over the recording. Next, she created a application that presented a written version of the poem on the computer screen. A student could read the poem and click the mouse on any obscure words to see their definitions, or to learn more about Dylan Thomas or the significance of this particular poem. By selecting a region of text ranging from a single word to the entire poem, the user can also hear Dylan Thomas reading the selection. The addition of this audio capability – hearing the great poet reading his work in the highest quality audio reproduction possible, multiplies the power of her application.

Making your own applications

Voyager has created an HyperCard authoring aid (CD Audio Stack) for Mac owners who want to make their own indexed audio applications. Students can master this product quickly, and can easily create their own programs to explore any music disk they have at hand. Apple IIGS owners can do the same with HyperStudio using Roger Wagner's XCommands disk.

As an example of the kinds of projects students might create, I took a CD of the Bach two- and three part inventions and used CD Audio Stack to create buttons that played the inventions. These buttons were pasted on HyperCard cards describing each of the pieces.

Bach's Two-Part Inventions

The fragment shown above is from Bach's autograph of the eighth two-part invention – a playful piece in which the two voices chase each other as if they were playing a game.

Click to hear the invention

The ease with which I could bring CD-quality audio into my applications amazed me. It was a real challenge to stop working on this project and get to my other tasks!

Roll over Beethoven...

Warner New Media has released two CD-ROM titles

that are incredibly well done. Both are Mac-based explorations of classical music that combine powerful HyperCard stacks with CD-audio, but the ideas that underlie these products can be applied to any stacks you design on the Mac or on an Apple IIGS using HyperStudio.

The two works treated by Warner are Beethoven's 14th string quartet, and Mozart's Magic Flute.

The Beethoven CD contains a folder full of HyperCard stacks and 8 tracks of CD-audio covering the entire quartet and additional music used in various parts of the HyperCard applications. (The audio tracks can also be played on a traditional CD player, by the way.)

The first view...
When the program is first started, you are presented with several options. For example, if you want to listen to the quartet you can select one of four visual accompaniments to look at while listening. The first of these is a general discussion of the piece, and the remaining choices provide different types of analysis depending on your interest. For example, you can choose a harmonic analysis or one based on the detailed structure of the music. At any time, you can switch among the various analyses being presented by clicking your mouse on one of the numbers in the upper left corner of the screen.

⬚1⬚2⬚3⬚4⬚5 Harmonic Analysis – Movement 1   0:00 m1

First movement   Key: C-sharp minor

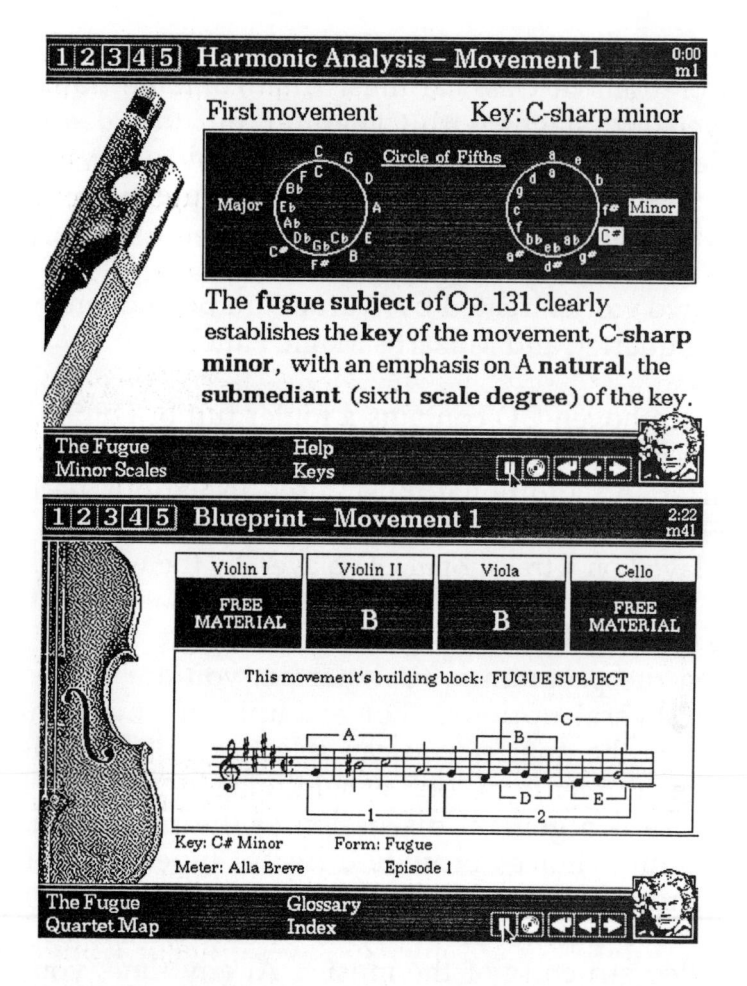

Circle of Fifths

Major / Minor

The **fugue subject** of Op. 131 clearly establishes the **key** of the movement, C-**sharp minor**, with an emphasis on A **natural**, the **submediant** (sixth **scale degree**) of the key.

The Fugue   Help
Minor Scales   Keys

⬚1⬚2⬚3⬚4⬚5 Blueprint – Movement 1   2:22 m41

Violin I	Violin II	Viola	Cello
FREE MATERIAL	B	B	FREE MATERIAL

This movement's building block: FUGUE SUBJECT

Key: C# Minor   Form: Fugue
Meter: Alla Breve   Episode 1

The Fugue   Glossary
Quartet Map   Index

The analysis keeps up with the music so your eyes are getting information that directly relates to what you are hearing.

Words in boldface have definitions available in small windows that appear by clicking the mouse on any of these special words. Additional topics of exploration are shown in the lower left corner of the screen. For example the first movement of the 14th string quartet is a fugue. If you want to know more about fugues, all you have to do is click the mouse on the word and you zoom into a small treatise on the topic that includes a description of the different parts of a fugue (including musical demonstrations). You can even hear portions of fugues by composers as diverse as Bach and Stravinsky.

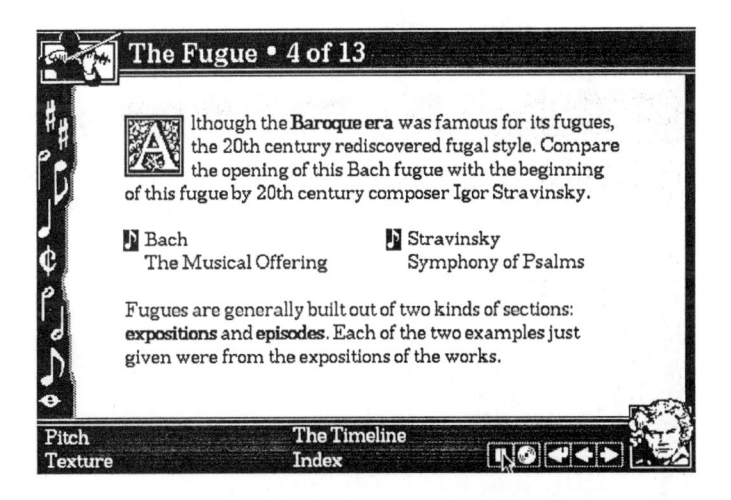

```
┌─────────────────────────────────────────────────────┐
│  The Fugue • 4 of 13                                │
│                                                     │
│     ┌──┐  lthough the Baroque era was famous for    │
│     │A │  its fugues, the 20th century rediscovered │
│     └──┘  fugal style. Compare the opening of this  │
│     Bach fugue with the beginning of this fugue by  │
│     20th century composer Igor Stravinsky.          │
│                                                     │
│     ♪ Bach                    ♪ Stravinsky          │
│        The Musical Offering      Symphony of Psalms │
│                                                     │
│     Fugues are generally built out of two kinds of  │
│     sections: expositions and episodes. Each of the │
│     two examples just given were from the           │
│     expositions of the works.                       │
│                                                     │
│  Pitch              The Timeline                    │
│  Texture            Index                           │
└─────────────────────────────────────────────────────┘
```

If your interest runs more along the lines of historical context, you can summon a time line of classical music and see brief biographies of several major composers (with samples of some of their music).

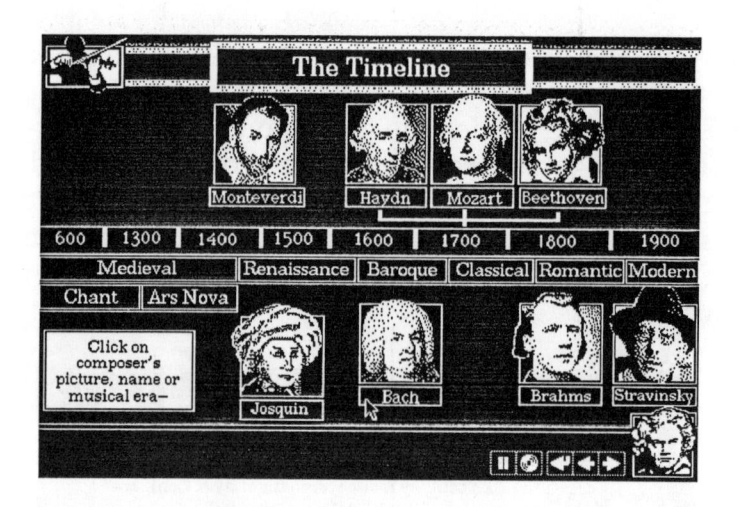

Another branch takes you to a section on Beethoven's deafness in which you can hear how his music might have sounded to him at various periods in his life.

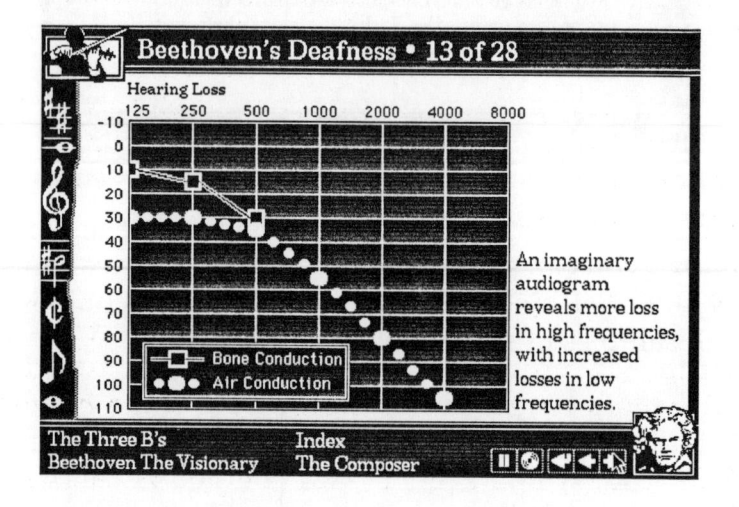

An imaginary audiogram reveals more loss in high frequencies, with increased losses in low frequencies.

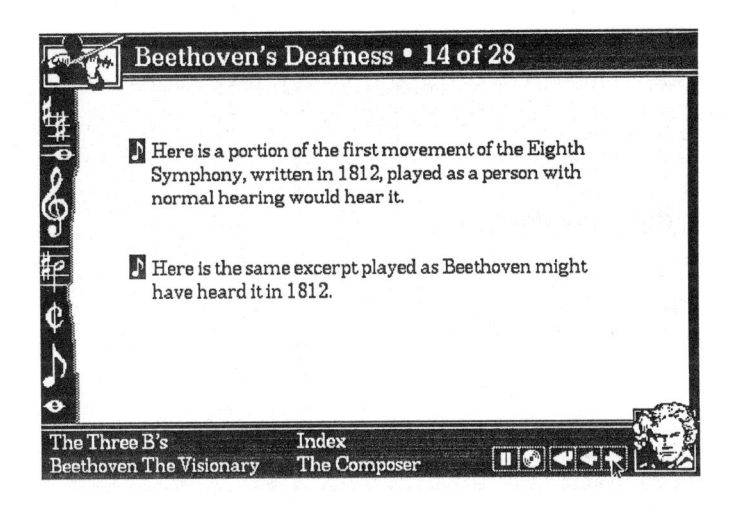

> **Beethoven's Deafness • 14 of 28**
>
> ♪ Here is a portion of the first movement of the Eighth Symphony, written in 1812, played as a person with normal hearing would hear it.
>
> ♪ Here is the same excerpt played as Beethoven might have heard it in 1812.
>
> The Three B's Index
> Beethoven The Visionary The Composer

This one CD-ROM application is so flexible that I can't imagine two people using it the same way. Aside from the incredible scholarship represented in this product, the HyperCard stacks are crafted in a way that supports numerous learning styles. For example, the linguistic learner might prefer the written descriptions of the music while the spatial learner might prefer looking at the blueprint of the piece. One of the attractions of this application is that many of the user's intelligences are engaged at the same time.

What does it mean?
Instructional design for lecture-based delivery is (or should be) incredibly different from that based on multimedia-based exploration of the same content. Lectures progress in linear fashion from start to finish, while student interactions with computers can be far more open ended.

Lectures and books fit well together because they are both linear media. While humans have learned to adapt to this format (except, perhaps, for the 700,000 students who drop out each year), most of the research on learning styles and the functioning of the brain seems to indicate that we naturally operate in a more holistic fashion. Young children, left to their own devices, become engaged in one topic, shift to another point of view, change topics all together, and learn in ways that engage all the senses. It is only on entering school that most childrens' rate of learning undergoes a rapid decline.

The logistics of cost effective classrooms have typically required that one human being try to instruct 30 or more children at a time. The invention of lectures and books made this task possible, even though this approach is less than optimal for most of us.

The Beethoven and Mozart disks support a more natural way of learning – one that specifies the content to be covered, and also supports multiple views of this content. If we view the Beethoven quartet as a region of conceptual space, then the Warner CD-ROM becomes a navigational tool with which we can chart our own course through this piece of music. We have our choice of tour guides and a good body of reference materials close at hand if we want to extend our exploration into territories unfamiliar to us.

Of course, programs with this depth of content are very expensive to produce. Few of us can support several university professors for 18 months while they provide the background research for a single piece of music.

On the other hand, if we empower students to be the constructors of their own knowledge, the Warner series (which will also be expanding their titles into the contemporary music domain) can serve as a model for applications created by students themselves in any area of academic interest.

As a teacher, you can determine the content – the region of conceptual space to be explored by the class – and then allow students to create their own applications that let you (or anyone else, for that matter) navigate through this space from the student's perspective. By using the students' map yourself, you'll have a good idea of their mastery of the content.

However, for any of this to have an impact on education, teachers must be willing to move from the paradigm of lecture-based instruction to one in which they serve as catalysts and facilitators of student-based learning – they have to be willing to move from teacher-based instruction to student-based construction of content. If you are willing to try this idea in even one subject, you will have forever changed the concept of education in the minds of your students.

Video Games and Informal Education

For many, school is a place of hard wooden seats and harsh fluorescent lighting – a place where I have a hard time imagining education being an engaging activity. Now place a teacher in this room who is presented as the font of all wisdom and who likes to dispense this wisdom word by word as the clock ticks to measure out a curriculum designed by administrators and legislators who may spend an entire career without working in a classroom themselves. What a depressing image!

It seems to me that if we are to learn anything from the students who drop out of school each year, it is that many of our schools, by their very structure, fail to reinforce and develop the natural love of learning each child seems to express on the first day of Kindergarten.

Perhaps if we explore an informal learning environment in which students appropriate their own knowledge, we might get some ideas we can apply in the traditional classroom.

Follow your bliss
The best learning takes place when the student is engaged. One of the most stunning examples of this phenomenon is the continued success of video games. When this "fad" started many years ago with such classics as Pong and Breakout, many predicted the

rapid demise of the genre. But when video games failed to die, some opponents decried the violent nature of some games and even went so far as to suggest that they be banned or restricted as if they were pornographic. In the meantime, video games continued to thrive and some of the non-violent games have become classics.

I believe that by looking at some of these games we can gain some insights of value to formal education. One of the unquestionably great games of the decade is Tetris – an abstract geometric game that grew out of the creator's interest in pentominos. Tetris was designed by the Russian mathematician, Alexey Pajitnov – a researcher in artificial intelligence and speech recognition at the USSR Academy of Sciences. In addition to the arcade version of this game, Spectrum Holobyte has published Apple II versions for the 64K, 128K and Apple IIGS platforms, as well as for other computer systems.

The principle of the game is simple. The player is presented with a falling game piece composed of four squares arranged in one of six randomly chosen patterns. This piece can be rotated and moved horizontally as it drops to the bottom of the screen. The object is to place the pieces so that they fill a horizontal row. When each row is filled, it disappears from the screen, making room for more layers of pieces. The game is over when pieces pile up to the top of the screen. At each level of play the falling speed increases, thus requiring faster decision making on the part of the player.

This game, which has been called the Rubik's Cube of software, engages thousands of players whose teachers say "can't concentrate on math." I'm amazed to see high school students struggling in a math classroom who then go to the arcade and consistently score in the top 10 as they play this highly spatial and logical math puzzle for hours on end. In talking with these players it is interesting to observe the depth of their problem-solving and logical thinking ability. Complex strategies are created to deal with various game situations. These strategies must be recalled and acted upon very quickly. This development and testing of hypotheses is a critical component of mathematical thinking, and it is commonplace among Tetris players.

Contrast the knowledge developed by the student in playing Tetris with that presented by a teacher who drones on from the front of the class, spoon feeding mathematical ideas devoid of context or meaning to the students who must stay in their seats or be punished.

Video games in the classroom?
Does this mean that I think video games should be brought to class? My only reason for hesitating to say yes has nothing to do with the value of playing games like Tetris or an older favorite of mine, Qix. My fear is that the simple placement of game machines in the classroom might absolve some teachers of their responsibility to assist in the engagement of the student in a way that develops and maintains the true love of learning with which we are all born.

I challenge any math teacher to play just one game of

Tetris (or Pajitnov's newer games, Welltris or Faces). I don't think it can be done – the games are just too engaging!

Another way to think about engagement is to think in terms of intrinsic motivation. Intrinsic motivation is central to lifelong learning – you need to have your own motivation to master any subject in a meaningful way. The self-imposed choice to pit yourself against a video game appears in sharp contrast to challenges imposed purely from the outside with no attempt to connect the content with the student. In the first case the student's mind is fully engaged, and in the second it is likely to be shut down with fear or boredom.

Of course it might be argued that the "instructional content" of Tetris isn't relevant to the subject being taught and that arguments pertaining to the "transferability" of this game are tenuous at best. But, while there might be some merit to this argument, the fact remains that many students who (in the eyes of their teachers) have no grasp of math, are actually quite proficient at the subject when they are able to approach it on their own terms.

Dr. Joyce Norman at California State University in Chico, California studied mathematical problem solving with a large group of teenagers. Students were divided into two groups and were given the same math test. Students in one group could take as long as they liked to finish it, and the other group had to finish the test in one hour. When time was not a factor, the distribution of scores was the same for boys and girls. But for the timed tests, the average score for boys was higher than that for girls. In follow up interviews it was found that girls had a greater tendency to solve the problems linguistically and that boys had a greater tendency to solve them spatially. Because spatial problem solving is generally much faster than linguistic problem solving, the performance difference could be understood.

The relevance of this study to video games is easy to see. Students who develop spatial problem solving ability by playing video games have a math test advantage over those who do not develop those skills. Many video games (such as the GameBoy by Nintendo) perpetuate the illusion of electronic games as purely masculine activities. If we bring video games into the classroom, we can provide gender equity and help to improve spatial problem solving abilities in all our students.

Experiments by Dr. Pat McClurg at the University of Wyoming have shown that exposure to computer-based spatial problem solving software (such as Factory from Sunburst Communications) transfers to significantly increased student ability in solving spatial problems of all kinds.

The classroom revisited

One of the major applications of educational computing for "at risk" students centers around integrated learning systems – lab-based rows of computers at which students bask in the dim glow of monitor light while their brains are crammed full of piecemeal knowledge using techniques that would have George Orwell doing cartwheels in his grave.

Whenever I see a room of students being programmed by these machines my mind flashes to the plight of veal calves who spend their lives cramped in dimly lit pens too small for them even to stand as they are brought to slaughter weight on a diet of bland fluid.

Of course the purveyors of integrated learning systems (from whom I will no doubt be hearing) make their point that students using their material do increase their test scores. I don't doubt that – the veal calves gain weight on their diet also. But is this what education is all about? Where does wonder fit in? How about true understanding? Does joy have a place? What is the benefit of being able to identify a verb if you can't see the beauty in a Dylan Thomas poem? And, do the tests these students take measure the skills we need to thrive in the twenty-first century?

Tetris may not improve one's performance on a math test (although my hunch is it will) but in its own way it does reveal a bit of the beauty lurking in geometry as they player finds ways to fill gaps in a line with a random assortment of pieces.

Beauty and relevance is the key
Every subject taught in school has, at its base, relevance and beauty. Teachers who can't give immediate examples of this to their students have no business in the profession. When a student says, "Why are we learning this?" the question is a plea for help in finding the relevance and beauty in the topic. If the teacher can only say, "You need to know this because it will be on the test," or "This will help you later in life," (without providing specific examples)

this teacher has failed the student in a fundamental way by saying, in effect, "I'm only teaching this because it is my job."

On the other hand, the teacher who can point to the relevance and beauty of the subject has the capacity to engage the student in his or her personal quest for knowledge. The personal computer, with its almost infinite capacity to model and portray microworlds, is a perfect tool to enlist in the engagement of all learners.

What we need are more educational software developers willing to bring the same level of fascination and engagement to curriculum-based software that the game designers bring to the arcades.

After all, a computer is a terrible thing to waste.

The Hacker Mentality in Education

The term "hackers" has been popularized as a way of characterizing some computer users who seemingly spend their entire lives bathed in the glow of a computer display screen. These people go without sleep and bathing, subsisting on Jolt cola and Twinkies as they fathom the depths of the latest computer game, or find entry to yet another computer network. While the term hacker used to be synonymous with "nerd," hackers are known more for their single mindedness of purpose than for their unkempt appearance and occasional lack of social graces.

In the last few years, hackers acquired a better reputation as a group. To start with, some of them became multi-millionaires, took a bath and started wearing shoes. Also, their dedication to the pursuit of knowledge, even if it was in the limited realm of computers, stood in stark positive contrast to those youth who choose instead to drop out and who fill the emptiness of their lives with drugs.

As I look at the challenges facing education today, it seems to me that we need more hackers – not just computer hackers of course, but hackers in all areas of knowledge. We need to find ways to keep kids' intrinsic love of learning alive well into high school so that it never gets lost. The child who gets lost in a good book has much in common with the child who plays Tetris for hours on end – they are both engaged in activities filled with the opportunity to learn and to develop skills. The poet who stays up all night searching for the perfect word, the songwriter crafting a fine melody and the anthropologist piecing together the shreds of a lost civilization are all hackers. They are wedded to their muses. To get lost in the vast universe of ideas and to create one's own map of these uncharted territories has got to be one of the most powerful capabilities of the human intellect.

If you accept that history hackers exist, along with hackers in every other domain of human knowledge, then we can see why we should have more hackers in education.

To start with, hackers are self motivated – they spend significant parts of their lives engaged in their passion for no reason other than the pleasure it provides. If the hacker is rewarded with money (or grades), then so much the better; but it is the true love of the thing that captures the hacker's spirit and keeps him or her entranced.

Second, many hackers were introduced to their passion by others – they didn't all find it on their own. This suggests that teachers can play a significant role by helping students understand why the subjects they teach have the potential for excitement. Starting from this base, it is more likely that others will be enticed to see pleasure in a field previously associated with drudgery.

Third, the hacker is likely to chart his or her own course through a subject. He or she may start at too high a level and then have to backtrack. If you're a teacher of someone learning in this fashion, you'll be expected to be a resource for solutions, not a critic of paths chosen. By the way, this also implies that the hacker will develop proficiencies far beyond our expectations – after all, the subject under study has become an overriding passion.

A problem with all of this is that it depends almost entirely on the student's own motivation. What are we to do with the student who develops a passion for math at the total exclusion of writing, for example – or, worse yet, the student who has become so turned off to school that he or she finds nothing of interest? And, with students operating at their own pace in a variety of subjects, how can we insure that the required curriculum is covered in the prescribed period of time?

Well, of course, we can't make any guarantees. But we must remember that the current educational agenda in our country is derived from an industrial-age model of education in which the human mind is seen more as a vessel to be filled than as a fire to be kindled. Vessel filling is manageable; it is measurable, and it is under the control of a teacher. The only problem with it is that it doesn't give students very much of utility in their lives. Yes there are some exceptions – math facts, vocabulary development, and other topics that require a base of factual knowledge will still be important in the future. But unless these topics are presented in context and are integrated with subjects that ignite passion in our students, we risk failing our future.

As for the student who lacks interest in all academic subjects, we need to intervene with these students early enough to keep this from happening. I'm convinced that some of our brightest students mentally tune out of education because, deep down, they know that their subjects deserve a far better treatment than they receive in many classrooms.

One of the early justifications for educational computing was that it allowed students to learn at their own pace. Now, with the increased availability of multimedia in the classroom, technology allows students to work in their own learning styles as well. And yet for all the lip service that we paid to this topic since the late 1970's, we still have yet to provide meaningful access to computers to our students.

Furthermore, many computer-intensive schools have rooms equipped with so-called integrated learning systems that promise improved test results by cramming information into a child (providing, typically, only short term improvement in performance). I'd rather see computers used "less efficiently" by students who create their own measurement apparatus with Brøderbund's Science Toolkit, or who plot complicated math functions with a program they have written themselves in Applesoft BASIC.

Rather than predigest a curriculum and remove all the risk and uncertainty from it, students should be presented with open-ended challenges that they must solve themselves. This not only builds their self-esteem, it helps kindle the fire that we see burning in the eyes of intrepid hackers everywhere – a fire that illuminates the love of learning that is the hallmark of a truly educated person.

Kid's Computing Comes of Age

Do you remember when the first pocket calculators came out? As I recall, they sold for a few hundred dollars. At that time the world was filled with bulky mechanical monsters and the calculator market, according to the market researchers, was not going anywhere. It was thought that people would replace their mechanical clunkers with the new electronic marvels, but no growth was predicted beyond that.

Suddenly, when calculators broke the $10 barrier, the market blew wide open. Now you can get a decent solar powered calculator for under five bucks – including tax.

Dead Mice Smell Bad

I want to make a point about educational technology with this example, so let's call calculators "number processors" for what follows. When number processors were expensive, no one much worried about their role in education. After all, if students couldn't afford these tools, then we'd better keep teaching them how to do long division by hand. Of course, the advent of the truly low-cost calculator has changed all this. There isn't a child in school who can't afford to have his or her own calculator. For the one-time price of a school supplied hot lunch, even the poorest of students can let modern technology remove the drudgery from what is really a beautiful science. Instead of teaching kids how to do rote long division (divide, multiply, subtract, bring down, or "dead mice smell bad"), we can be helping kids to identify the kinds of problems that call for division in the first place and can help them learn to quickly estimate the answer in their heads.

Even so, there are pitifully few school programs in this country built around the notion that each child has (or should have) his or her own electronic number processor.

As one neo-Luddite teacher said to me, "What will the child do when the batteries go dead?" When I patiently explained that solar powered calculators don't use batteries, she then said, "Well suppose you need to do a calculation in the dark."

Sure.

When is the last time you were in a house that lost power in the middle of the night because of a hurricane and someone said, "How much is 786 divided by 27?"

The low cost of number processors is helping identify the real challenge in educational technology – getting people to accept that we live in an era different from the one in which we grew up.

I mention the "calculator in the classroom" battle because, I'm seeing another philosophical war looming on the horizon.

Personal Word Processing
This chapter is being written on a plane somewhere over the California coast using a word processor built

into the Laser PC-3 computer. If you haven't seen this computer (or its more versatile brother, the PC-4), it weighs about a pound, runs for ages on four penlight cells, has 32K of RAM, a built-in spell checker, calculator, communications package and a bunch of other programs I haven't even tried yet. Its only drawback as a word processor is the two-line display that shows only 20 characters per line. (The PC-4 has a quieter keyboard and has a 4 line display of 40 characters per line.)

This computer has a full-sized keyboard (similar to the one on the Apple IIc), yet is about the size of a hardback book.

The best news is its price. For about $150 ($250 for the PC-4) you get the computer plus the software for your desktop machine needed to port your text to your main computer and a complete set of cables for serial file transfer and to connect a parallel printer.

Years ago I pleaded with Apple to create an inexpensive laptop that children could own – a computer that could be used under the shade of a tree, at a desk in school or home, or in the car on the way to Aunt Gertrude's for the holidays. I envisioned this computer being universally available. (Yes, that means that every school-aged child in the country would have one.)

Well, that time is coming, even if the label isn't going to be Apple's.

When I got back to my office I transferred this file onto

my desktop computer and tweaked it with my word processor – just as I'd expect kids to do when they have their own notebook-sized computers.

The classroom computer can and should have all the bells and whistles. Kids should be able to upload their material into a computer with a high quality display for refinement, but they don't need those features to capture their ideas in the first place.

But what about the cost?
Now I know that, just as with early number processors, this word processor will be "too expensive" to provide to every child. But think about this. If I could buy a computer with the file transfer software for my desktop machine AND two interface cables for $150, what would the computer cost by itself?

Also, remember that I only bought one. My guess is that the dealer margin is high enough that I could probably get the computer (by itself) in quantity for under $100.

If that's true, then what do you think I could get it for if I represented a school district who wanted 16,000 of these puppies?

My guess is that we will quickly approach the time when a computer with the power of the PC-4 could be put into the hands of every kid in the country for $50, and still leave enough incentive for some manufacturer to create the things.

Let's see now, fifty bucks times 100 million kids, that's

about $5 billion. These days, that's about what we spend propping up the Kingdom of Spudonia.

Because notebook computers like those made by Laser and Tandy can port text to our Apple II's and other computers, and document creation is such a major task that it warrants its own computer, true compatibility is not an issue (even though I'm still hoping for an Apple II laptop that has the price and performance of the low-cost MS-DOS laptops I've seen.)

Sharpened any quills lately?
I leave it to Laser, Tandy and the other makers of notebook computers to decide who wants this phenomenally large market. I'm more concerned with the likely response from those educators who are still resisting calculator use in the classroom.

"But children won't learn good penmanship," or "With a spell checker they won't need to know how to spell pneumonia."

Right; but with each child having his or her own computer, maybe we can get to the real purpose of writing – expressing ideas in a form by which they can be effectively communicated to others.

I know one child who would be helped immediately by having one of these computers. She's a tremendously creative fourth-grader whose everyday speech is filled with rich metaphor. The child is a born storyteller. She's also tremendously dysgraphic, even though she can read quite well. Still, her d's sometimes look like b's, or g's, or q's, and writing is a painful experience for her. For a child with her rich imagination and flair for writing to be denied access to a low-cost word processor is tantamount to child abuse.

There's only one way I know how to become a good writer – and that is to do a lot of writing. When writing is a physically painful task (as it becomes for the student who clings to his pen so hard that it leaves marks in his hand), and when student manuscripts have to be completely recopied by hand with each revision, the chance to entice good ideas from children disappears.

Yes, when I was young I didn't have these fancy tools. In fact, my desk had an inkwell in it. But we are not living in my or anyone else's past. A $50 computer lighter than a dictionary should be in the book bag of every kid in the country. Period.

Computers and Testing

Management consultant Tom Peters says "What gets measured gets done." This applies to education as much as it does to industry. In fact, it might be more accurate to suggest that, in education, what gets tested gets taught.

We are in the midst of a major restructuring effort in education in this country, yet this effort can be thwarted if we don't change our tests to conform to the new curriculum and objectives of education. To see why, let's say that you replaced your science textbook-based lectures with student projects in which teams built HyperCard or HyperStudio stacks on various animals that were then shared with the rest of the class. Student enthusiasm for science would probably skyrocket, and students might learn some things that were not covered in the traditional curriculum. By the same token, some information might be left out.

Even though the whole experience was beneficial, and students learned more that they will remember about animals, these students might do poorly on a test based on the content covered in the textbook. A teacher would then conclude (incorrectly) that the new curriculum was not effective and revert to rote lectures to improve student test performance.

Any restructuring of the curriculum requires an immediate change in the nature and the content of the assessment tools used to measure the effectiveness of the program. Yet, all too often, we insist on measuring student performance with tests that have little or no relevance to changes in the manner and content of instruction.

None of the above...

The majority of tests administered at the school-wide to nation-wide level are multiple choice examinations in which students shade in circles or rectangles with a number 2 pencil to register their answer. No room is allowed for student explanations of his or her choice. The advantage of this type of examination is that it is inexpensive to administer and score. The student's "bubble" sheets can be fed into a simple scanner and the results of thousands of tests can be determined in a few minutes. We have become so used to this type of examination that many of us have become blind to its limitations.

Based on scores from these tests, we conclude that our nation lags others in math ability, etc. In response to this gap, providers of integrated learning systems (ILS) promise districts that their software will let students improve their test performance by plugging themselves into a personal computer cocoon as the ILS software programs the students to answer the kinds of questions found on standardized tests. While short term improvement in test scores can be achieved with these programs, student attitudes toward the subject matter usually suffer as a result. This isn't a concern, however, since student attitude toward mathematics isn't measured by the standardized tests.

What gets lost in the quest for improved test scores, is that the ILS programs are designed to mimic the structure of the tests with little regard for helping students develop any meaningful relationship with the subject matter. If the tests are designed to treat the child as a repository of disconnected facts, then this software is prepared to treat the child as a vessel to be filled with context-free information – garbage in, garbage out.

The development of an inexpensive grading technology (computer scanned bubble sheets) has had far reaching impact on our curriculum and, secondarily, on student attitudes toward learning. As long as our priorities are "cost effectiveness" rather than meaningful education, any attempts at educational reform are doomed.

Another approach...

The picture need not be so bleak, however, if we examine the function of our tests and take advantage of the modern technology sitting in most of our classrooms. First, it seems to me that a school should only administer a test if the test measures things that are valued by the school. If a school cares about dropout rates, for example, measures of student attitude are more important than measures of math proficiency, yet very few schools try to measure this affective component of education.

Second, the tests need to allow the student to display evidence of his/her thinking process, not just the ability to produce an answer. To see why, consider the following question (taken from a new test under development):

Can you construct a right triangle with internal angles of 90, 60 and 20 degrees? Why or why not?

One student correctly stated that the triangle could not be constructed, but explained his reasoning as follows: "This triangle can't be built because $20^2 + 60^2 \neq 90^2$."

In other words, the student saw three numbers and blindly applied the Pythagorean theorem to this problem, even though this response was totally incorrect. On a multiple choice test, this student would have been given credit, even though his math was severely flawed.

Of course, one argument against open-ended questions is that they can't be machine graded. This is true, perhaps, but it is time we put the student's knowledge ahead of the economics of test grading. The function of an assessment, after all, is to measure the things we value, not to be cheap.

Computers to the rescue...

If we are serious in our quest to track student performance in meaningful ways, what could be better than a portfolio of work selected by the student as representative of his/her best efforts. While this portfolio might get quite bulky by the end of 12 years, it would provide a meaningful glimpse of a student's development through his/her school years.

As personal computers become more commonplace in the classroom, the bulk of a portfolio can be reduced by keeping writing samples and other materials on disks. In addition to being more manageable than paper, disk-based portfolios can be searched more easily, and copies can be made for distribution to colleges or other institutions wanting to see transcripts of a student's work.

To see one example of a student-based assessment tool, imagine a HyperCard or HyperStudio stack for a class in which each card in the stack contains a digitized picture of a child. Next to this picture are three buttons: My Goal, My Progress to December, and My Progress to June. By clicking on each button, the user can hear the child's own voice reciting his/her major academic goal for the year, progress to the end of the semester, and progress to the end of the year. In addition to being a wonderful tool to share with parents, this stack can become part of a permanent record that can be examined years into the future.

In the academic domain, one can envision computer simulations of science experiments in which students are provided with a scenario and are allowed to interact with the simulation in ways that produce the desired result. The computer can keep track of the choices made by the student, and can assess student proficiency as the task is being completed. This interactive use of technology provides immediate feedback and, except for the cost of the computer workstations, is economically viable for a wide range of subject areas ranging from language arts to history, math and science. The ability of the computer to keep journals of student comments provides the opportunity for open-ended assessments that are impossible with bubble sheeted tests.

It is easy to think of many ways that personal computers can be used to put a human face on assessment of student performance. Until we break away from our reliance on inhumane multiple choice tests that fail to measure the skills we want our children to have, educational restructuring will fail, and we will have failed the needs of an entire generation of children.

Renaissance II – an Afterword

I started this book by suggesting that Leonardo da Vinci was frustrated because, in his day, technology was not advanced enough to allow the implementation of his ideas. Now let's look at his era from another perspective. The time of the Italian Renaissance was one in which people were free to think grand thoughts – to make discoveries and to create classic works of art, music, poetry and science that we still enjoy today.

This Renaissance came about for several reasons. First, the flourishing commerce of Florence brought great wealth and leisure opportunities to families, allowing them to pursue other studies. Second, the rise of the celebration of human life encouraged curiosity in areas that had been hidden since the time of Classical Greece. A society hungry for knowledge not only searched far and wide for the wisdom of older civilizations, it made discoveries of its own.

Many of the discoveries we marvel at today were made by people expert in several fields. This expertise led them to be able to bring advances to subjects through avenues that were previously unexplored. For example, interest in the science of anatomy helped people like Leonardo become better figure artists. The same can be said for the impact of the mathematics of perspective on Renaissance art in general.

The term, "Renaissance person" applies to anyone who has a broad range of interests that cut across several domains of study. The painter, Raphael, for example, was also an architect and mathematician. Leonardo was a military engineer, artist, essayist, writer of children's stories, and a consummate inventor (among many other things).

If the first Renaissance was a result of wealth and leisure, the second Renaissance will arise from different needs. I believe that we are at the door of Renaissance II – a second flowering of broad interest in intellectual pursuits that cuts across many subject areas. Furthermore, unlike the first Renaissance, this one will apply to all of society, and especially to our children. Second, participation in this Renaissance is not a result of idle curiosity, it is instead the key to our economic and social survival.

Lifelong learning was a luxury in the 16th century, but it is a survival skill today. Here's why.

As Alvin Toffler (and others) have told us, human development has been marked by periods, or ages, that have shaped the structure of society. The agricultural age, for example, lasted about 6000 years. It was followed by the industrial age which dominated society for only 300 years. According to Lynch and Kordis (in their book, Strategy of the Dolphins), the current age of information may dominate for only 30 years before it too is supplanted by still other ages. Lynch and Kordis suggest that we are at the brink of the productivity age, and that it will be followed by the age of imagination, with still others to follow.

It is important to keep in mind that new ages do not completely displace old ones. Agriculture continues to be important today, as it will for the duration of our species. The same can be said for industry. We will always need the ability to produce manufactured goods.

What this suggests is that, as each age comes into view, we are being given another ball to juggle. Our dominant interest may be taken up by the "age du jour," but some part of our society is still operating with all the other ages we have ever had. The ability to live in a world with numerous simultaneous frameworks is one challenge facing our students.

Another challenge comes from the rapidity of change. Our parents and grandparents had periods of their lives in which the prevailing world view stayed constant for a long time. We and the children we teach do not have this luxury. Instead we are being bombarded by increasingly rapid change until we reach the point where "flux" will become the new flow.

I consider it interesting that management consultant Tom Peters went from "Searching for Excellence" to "Thriving on Chaos" in less than ten years. As he says in the latter book, the changes we have been waiting for have already happened, and the pace of continued change is increasing with no end in sight.

It seems to me that there are two likely outcomes from increased rates of change in society – unbridled chaos, or the opportunity for phenomenal growth and development. The path that is chosen depends on several factors. First, if we adopt a "victim" mentality in which we see ourselves as being blown around by forces out of our control, then we will get sucked into whirlpools of despair and our entire country will fast become a replica of inner-city Detroit – a burned out testimony to the failure of the human spirit.

If, on the other hand, we see ourselves as proactive participants in the creation of our own future, we can harness the hurricane forces of change and direct them in ways that lead to a higher quality of life for all our people.

Central to this second choice is a strong sense of individual capability. One of the best ways to foster this sense of capability is to help our students retain their innate love of learning – to have it grow and become a lifelong passion. As my friend, Ian Jukes, says; "We don't need to be fire kindlers, we need to become arsonists."

Here are some thoughts on how to accomplish this:

1. Our goal should be construction, not instruction – finding ways to help students become the appropriators of their own knowledge, because it empowers and excites students and prepares them for lifelong learning.

2. Educators should model domains of knowledge as "conceptual space" in which learners can build their own maps and conduct their own explorations. These maps are the means by which educators can assess student progress, and they can be built in many ways. Just as a map to your house might contain written directions, or it

might be a drawing, music might be thought of as a map of feelings. Basically, maps can be created using any or all of the seven multiple intelligences we discussed earlier in this book. The beauty of using multimedia technology in map creation is that it supports multiple views of the same space. The Beethoven CD-ROM application described earlier is a splendid example of this.

If we adopt a model of the student as constructor of knowledge, the role of technology in facilitating this process is easy to see. Meaningful educational software development will be done by the students themselves. We, the teachers, will then be the users of the students' software as we use it to see how well they have mastered their subjects.

In addition to changing our role with students, our task as educators is to become passionate learners ourselves – to stretch our own thoughts and capabilities in new directions. I believe that every teacher should be on a quest for development of the intellect – to be able to write a poem, a computer program, play a musical instrument, dance, paint a picture, create a new meal, prove a theorem, and know something about science. Furthermore, I think our children should be able to do the same.

Unless we see ourselves as lifelong learners, it will be nearly impossible to infuse this mindset in our children. Too many of today's youth are being raised by parents who see their own lives in terms of limitations, and who spread this same dismal view to their kids. Parents of my generation pushed for excellence in education, had high expectations for their children, and supported teachers in any way they could. Yet, today, I see many parents who tell teachers to "lighten up" on their kids, rather than help their children be all they can be.

We need to be strong in the face of such pressure. We need to fight for excellence, for a demanding curriculum, for opportunities for children to stretch their thinking beyond the expectations of the curriculum. We need to create environments in which children have furrowed brows – where they are confronted with questions without easy answers, questions that form the basis for research projects that cut across the boundaries of traditional disciplines. We need, above all, to provide safe environments in which students are free to explore and make mistakes without fear of ridicule. We need to acknowledge that children are born problem solvers, and that, given the chance, they can tackle real problems and produce practical results.

We need to design and implement assessments that encourage students to treat the content of instruction as the starting point, not the ending point, of knowledge.

As an example of one such setting, we are helping to design a thematic curriculum in which students in Monterey, California will work alongside research scientists as they try to salvage the environmentally threatened Monterey dunes.

Thematic projects of this type are springing up all over the country, and student participants are so excited about their education that they show up at school an hour before the building opens, and almost have to be forcibly removed at night.

Public schools in our country are incredibly underutilized resources. In most classrooms students arrive at the last possible moment, and dash out as soon as they are able. As an alternative, imagine school being a place where students, teachers and the public at large wanted to be. Schools like this exist, and they have a transformative effect on their communities.

The second Renaissance will have many advantages over the first. Advances in multimedia technology are bringing us to the point where Walt Disney's "If you can dream it, you can do it," vision will become the commonplace reality for all our children. Renaissance II will not happen by itself, however; it will require us to create it. As Apple Fellow Alan Kay (and others) have said, "The best way to predict the future is to invent it."

We are each the inventors of our own future. What I am asking is that each of us adopt a 20-year forward thinking perspective that we use as the basis for restructuring education. Our survival as a nation depends on our capacity to think in the future and act in the present. Then, and only then, will we be able to prepare children for their future, not for our past.

Glossary of Multimedia Terms

As multimedia technology becomes more commonplace, we will all start hearing terms that were once used mostly by engineers and other technical professionals. This brief glossary is intended to help you with these terms when you come across them.

Adapter: A device that permits interconnection of two connectors or devices that don't directly match.

ADC (Analog to Digital Converter): A device that converts an analog signal into its equivalent digital signal.

Algorithm: A set of calculations; normally a specific routine used by a programmer to complete a task.

Aliasing: The jagged, stair-stepped effect along the edges of computer graphics; also called "the jaggies."

Ambient: Light directed around rather than at the subject. Ambient noise is background or existing sounds at a location. Ambient air is the sound of a set or other location a its normal quiet level, as distinct from absolute silence.

Amplifier: A device that supplies power to and strengthens an incoming signal for output.

Analog: The variation of an electrical signal to represent the original image or sound that is being processed or reproduced.

Analog Film Recorder: A film recorder that registers the image as it comes from the computer screen and at the same resolution as the screen.

Analog Monitor: A display that uses an analog signal and displays an infinite number of shades of the primary colors or grayscale. Voltage varies continuously.

Animation: A process of creating movement of images on-screen.

ANSI (American National Standards Institute): The organization responsible for most standards used for U.S. audiovisual and computer equipment.

Anti-aliasing: An image-processing technique that reduces the appearance of aliasing on a graphics display. It makes the edges appear smoother and less sharp.

Aspect Ratio: In computer graphics, the ratio of the horizontal to vertical dimensions of a frame or image. The ability to maintain or control this ratio is important in the transfer and reproduction of an image for displays or for printed material.

ATR: Audio tape recorder.

Audio Signal: A varying voltage that carries information representing sound.

Audio Dub: Recording new audio on a tape after the

video has been shot. The dubbed audio records directly over one track of the original audio.

Audio mixing: Creating a custom audio track from several different sources using a sound mixing device.

Audiospace: Refers to the way sound can be manipulated to produce a particular audience impression.

Audio Track: The portion of a videotape that carries the audio signal.

Authorware: Development software programs that provide tools used to create interactive multimedia presentations, specifying elements – such as video and audio – that need to be included.

Bandwidth: The maximum frequency range of a signal, measured in hertz.

Beta: A 1/2" videotape format incompatible with the VHS format.

Bit: A single binary digit with a value of 0 or 1.

Bit Map Display: A display format in which the intensity or color of each point (pixel) on the screen corresponds to the value of a bit of computer memory.

BNC: A connector for coaxial cable (coax) that twists into place. BNC connectors are used for analog video signals in most semi-professional and professional video equipment.

Byte: A measure of computer data consisting of 8 bits of information. A single byte can have one of 256 possible values.

CAD (Computer Aided Design): In graphics, the computer-assisted production of drawings and plans.

Cardioid Microphone: A microphone that accepts sound in a somewhat heart-shaped sensitivity pattern. These microphones are very sensitive to sound coming from the front, and relatively insensitive to sound coming from the rear.

CAV (Constant Angular Velocity): In laser videodisk recordings, a format in which each frame takes exactly one track, allowing frame accurate freezing of the image.

CCD (Charge-coupled Device): A technology used in the light sensitive receptors found in most camcorders.

CD+G (Compact Disk Plus Graphics): A compact disk recording format that supports video as well as audio information. This format will find its niche in the entertainment market first.

CD-I (Compact Disk Interactive): A specification for an interactive product in which still images, computer graphics, audio and computer data are stored on one disk. This technology is starting to show up in the consumer entertainment market and it has great potential for education.

CD-ROM (Compact Disk Read Only Memory): A format standard for placing any kind of digital data on a compact disk. Typically, over 640 million bytes of data can be stored on a single CD-ROM.

CD-ROM XA (Compact Disk Read Only Memory Extended Architecture): Basically, a CD-I format with computer data, video and audio that has been designed for use as a computer peripheral.

Cel: A single drawing or frame in an animation.

Cel Animation: An animation technique in which the animated portions consist of a sequence of separate images that are shown in sequence.

CGA (Color Graphics Adapter): The first (and poorest) color video interface standard established for the IBM PC and compatibles.

Channel: A single audio signal path.

Character Generator: A device that electronically produces text displayed over a video image. Also called "Titlers."

Chasing: The process that occurs when a tape machine or sequencer changes its location to match that of another device.

Chroma (Chrominance): The amount and brightness of a hue as measured in the video signal. Without this signal, the video picture appears in black and white.

Chromakey: A method for inserting video images into other video backgrounds. The inserted image is videotaped against a colored background and the equipment replaces the colored background with the second video (background) image.

CLV (Constant Linear Velocity): In laser videodisk recordings, a format in which the disk rotates at varying speeds so the speed along each track is constant. This allows longer recording times (extended play), but does not allow freeze frame capabilities on most players.

Coax (Coaxial) Cable: A shielded cable used for video and low-level audio signals.

Color Bars: Standard color chart for adjusting the color balance in video equipment.

Color Cycling Animation: Changing the color mapping of pixels to create an animated image.

Colorization: Adding color to a black and white image, or changing colors in a color image.

Composite Video: A video output format in which the three color signals (red, green, blue) are combined with the timing (sync) signal into one composite signal that can be sent over one cable or broadcast through the airwaves. This is the format used when a VCR or some computers are connected to a video monitor.

Compression: A method by which video or audio signals can be stored or transmitted with much greater efficiency than the raw signal itself. Compression typically requires special equipment or programs.

Compressor: An audio signal processor that reduces the variation in the overall level of an audio signal.

Contrast Ratio: The ratio of brightness between the white and black areas of an image.

Convergence: Proper alignment of the vertical and horizontal lines, as in a video projector, for example.

Convert Utility: A program that allows the user to change one file format to another for use on different devices. The availability of these programs allows, for example, Macintosh and MS-DOS computer users to exchange text and picture files.

Copy Stand: A device for holding a video camera for shooting flat art or still items.

Crawl: The movement of credits or other graphic material across a video screen.

Cross Fade: An effect in which one sound or picture fades out while the next one fades in over it. Also called a cross dissolve.

CRT (Cathode Ray Tube): Type of display screen used to display text and graphics on most desktop computer systems and video monitors.

Cue Control: A device for rapidly advancing or rewinding a tape to sample the content or find a special area. Sometimes called a shuttle control.

Cut: An abrupt, instantaneous transition between two scenes in a production. Also slang for a video edit.

DAC (Digital Analog Converter: A device that converts digital signals used by the computer into analog signals. These devices are used in music and speech synthesizers, for example.

DAT (Digital Audio Tape): An audio recording format that produces CD-quality sound on special cassette tapes.

Decibel (dB): A measure of sound or signal intensity measured against a reference level.

Decoder/Encoder: A decoder translates a composite video signal into separate RGB signals. An encoder combines separate RGB signals into a composite video signal.

Definition: The sharpness or resolution of a picture.

Desktop Presentations: The use of computer-based multimedia tools to create presentations. The term can be used for everything from the design and printing of overhead transparencies to the production of interactive multimedia presentations involving a wide range of presentation equipment.

DIF (Data Interchange Format): A system that permits grabbing data from one program and bringing it into another.

Digital Audio: A format for audio recording in which the sound is recorded as a string of numbers that are used for the noise-free reconstruction of the sound.

Digital Monitor: A display that uses a digital signal and displays a more limited number of shades or gray levels than an analog monitor. Voltage varies in discrete steps.

Digitize: To capture an analog signal (video or sound) and convert it to digital form for storage and reconstruction in a computer, for example. The audio signals on CD's have been digitized. The CD player reconstructs the original audio using a DAC.

Digitizer: A device for converting analog signals to their digital counterparts. In computers, this term often refers to the capture of video signals.

Display size: The actual screen area of a monitor available for use. It is represented by the diagonal measure of the screen.

Dissolve: A short crossfade. A dissolve shot incorporates the fade of one image over another.

Dithering: In computer graphics, a method for blurring the transition from one color to another.

DOS (Disk Operating System): A program required to manage the hardware and logic resources of a computer.

Dot Pitch: A measure of the distance between dots on the monitor screen. The smaller the dot pitch, the denser the image appears.

Download: To transfer programs and/or data from one device to another. Also slang for making a "personal" copy of a tape.

Dropout: During playback, the instantaneous loss of a recorded signal due to imperfections in the tape.

Driver: A computer program used to control external devices or run other programs. CD-ROM drives, video disk player, and printers all require special driver programs to control them.

Drop Frame Time Code: SMPTE standard time code that drops frame number :00 and :01 each minute, except for every tenth minute, to compensate for NTSC variance from real clock time.

Dub: To copy a tape; also called "dupe."

Dump: To display, print or store the content of the computer memory. Also, the printing of a screen image.

DVI: A technology that allows a range of interactive products to deliver moving and still images, audio, dynamic graphics and computer data. A DVI disk is a CD-ROM with this special information on it. Compressed video footage can be expanded in real time (30 frames per second) on a personal computer.

Dynamic Range: The highest and lowest signal levels of a specific device.

Edit Controller: A device that controls two or more VCR's to accomplish smooth, accurate video editing.

EDL (Editing Decision List): A time-code list of edit points in a production. When the list is fed into a computerized edit controller, the EDL allows the system to auto-assemble the master tape from time-coded original raw footage.

EFP (Electronic Field Production): Used to describe the use of multiple camera setups on location. (See ENG.)

EGA (Enhanced Graphics Adapter): A color video interface standard developed after CGA.

EIA (Electronic Industries Association): The association that determines recommended video and audio standards in the United States.

Electronic Editing: Inserting or assembling program elements without physically cutting the tape.

Electronic Viewfinder: A small picture tube or LCD built into a video camera to allow the operator to see what is being scanned by the camera.

Emulation: To duplicate the behavior of a product or standard, as when an EGA adapter emulates CGA behavior.

ENG (Electronic News Gathering): Used to describe the

use of a single camera setup on location.

Enhance: The act of altering a basic image to conform to better design standards and visual understanding.

Erase Head: A separate head on an audio or video recorder that erases a previously taped signal before it is rerecorded.

Expansion Board: A plug-in circuit board that adds features to a computer.

Expansion Slots: The spaces in the computer to hold expansion boards.

Fade: A gradual increase or decrease of a video or audio signal. In video it is the appearance or disappearance from black; in audio it means decreasing or increasing volume from zero.

Fader: A sliding volume control that is used to adjust signal level.

Fat Bit Editing: The ability to magnify a portion of a computer image and edit it pixel by pixel.

FCC (Federal Communications Commission): The government agency in the United States that regulates the use of the airwaves for broadcasting.

Feedback: The regeneration of a signal when its output is fed back to the input. Audio feedback can cause "squeals." Video feedback (pointing the camera at the monitor) can produce interesting visual effects.

Field: One-half of a video frame, each consisting of 262 1/2 lines, each field being scanned in 1/60th of a second. One field scans the even lines, and the second scans the odd ones. (See interlace.)

Field Frequency: The number of fields per second. The NTSC field frequency is 60 per second, PAL is 50 per second.

Film Recorder: Device for creating slides or film prints of a video or computer graphics image.

Flutter: Rapid change in frequency of a video or audio signal due to variations in tape or disk speed.

Flying Erase Heads: Tape erasing heads in a VCR that erase the tape with frame accuracy, making perfect insert editing possible.

Foot Candle: The amount of light reflected by a surface one foot from a lighted candle. Metric equivalent is the lux.

Frame: A complete video image containing two interlaced video fields; 525 horizontal lines written in 1/30 second.

Frame Animation: An animation technique in which video images are recorded on film one frame at a time. The process is quite time consuming, but produces most of the high quality video seen in commercial titles for television programs, etc.

Frame Grabber: A device for capturing and storing a video frame from an external video source for display in a computer. Sometimes frame grabbers only grab one field.

Frequency Response: The frequency range over which signals are reproduced within a specified amplitude range. The frequency response of the human ear, for example, is from about 20 to 20,000 hertz (Hz.)

Front-screen Projection: An image projected on the audience side of a light-reflecting screen.

Full-motion Video: Video sequences that have enough images (30 frames per second) to impart smooth motion.

Genlock: A device that synchronizes one video source with another (e.g., computer graphics and video) for mixing and recording.

Gigabyte: One billion bytes. A CD-ROM holds 0.65 gigabytes of data.

Grab Utility: A RAM- or ROM-resident program that allows the user to capture a screen image from any program and save it on disk, or send it to a printer.

Graphic Equalizer: An audio device for adjusting sound quality by setting the gain at different frequency ranges. Graphic equalizers provide more options than simple treble and bass controls.

Grayscale: An even range of gray tones between black and white.

GUI (Graphical User Interface): An alternative to character-based computer interfaces such as MS-DOS. The Macintosh Finder and Microsoft Windows are two popular examples of GUI's.

HDTV (High-definition Television): Any of several proposed standards for higher resolution television approaching the quality of 35 mm slides.

Headroom: The difference between the optimal operating level of audio equipment and the "clipping" level at which distortion sets in. Consumer audio equipment typically has less headroom than professional equipment.

Hertz (Hz): Electronic measure of cycles per second.

Horizontal Blanking Interval: The time from the end of one horizontal scan to the start of the next. Other information can be sent during this time period.

Horizontal Resolution: The number of pixels available horizontally across the screen.

Horizontal Scan Rate: The speed at which the electron beam scans across a CRT. It is usually measured in kilohertz and ranges between 15 KHz and 40 KHz.

Hue: A single identifiable color, such as green.

Interface: The connection between two devices, such as

a computer and its peripherals.

Image Processing: Using software to manipulate a scanned video image. It is used to add colors, increase contrast at boundaries and produce other effects.

Image Recorder: A device that records digital signals and graphics to create, typically, 35 mm slides.

In-point: The starting point of an edit. (See out-point.)

Input/Output (I/O): The processes involved in transferring information into or out of a central processing unit.

Insert Editing: A video editing technique in which audio or video is inserted seamlessly into already recorded material. This requires a time code or control track on both the source and master video tape.

Interlace: A method of scanning used in video transmission in which each frame is divided into two interlaced fields to reduce flicker.

Jaggies: The jagged edges of shapes in computer graphics. Also called aliasing.

Jitter: Instability of an image due to sync or tracking problems.

Jump Cut: A jarring edit that creates a visual non sequitur, out of sync with the original.

Key: A special effect accomplished by electronically

cutting a hole in a video image and inserting another picture (see chromakey.) Keys are most often used for titles, but are seen on television weather reports all the time.

Kilobyte: 1024 bytes.

Kilohertz: 1000 hertz.

LAN (Local Area Network): A local network interconnecting computers, printers and other devices within an office.

Laser Videodisk: A video playback system that uses optical disks. Individual scenes or frames on a disk can be accessed directly or through computer control.

Lavalier: A small microphone worn on the lapel or under clothing.

LCD (Liquid Crystal Display): A popular technology used in flat panel display systems. Often used in portable computers, and also used for some video projectors.

LCD Panel: A video display designed to be set on a standard overhead projector for group viewing.

LD-ROM: A laser video disk (12" format) used to hold digital data.

Level: The intensity of an audio signal.

Level Matching: The process of insuring that the

outputs of one device are at the appropriate levels for the inputs of another device.

Level Meter: A device that provides an indication of the relative level of a audio signal.

Line Level: Refers to signals that are at or near the nominal operating level of an audio system.

Lumen: A measure of light emitted by a light source at the point of emission.

Luminance: The range from black through gray to white in a video picture.

Lux: A measure of light reflection. 1 lux is 1076 foot candles.

Master: The original video or audio recording.

Mastering Deck: A stereo recorder used to record the final mixed version of a multitrack production.

Matte: Method for creating composite pictures by placing a multicolored image from one video source over a background from a second source; a form of keying.

Megabyte (mb): 1 million bytes.

Mic Level: Refers to signals that are at the low levels produced by microphones. Mic level signals can be amplified to become line level signals.

MIDI (Musical Instrument Digital Interface): A standard for communicating information between synthesizers, sequencers, percussion machines, computers, and other electronic musical equipment.

MIDI Clock: A standard MIDI message that conveys one "click" of the sequencer clock. A MIDI clock has a rate of 24 times the quarter-note pulse.

MIDI Time Code: A portion of the MIDI standard that allows the SMPTE time code to be directly represented as MIDI messages that can be read by a computer or sequencer.

MIPS (Millions of Instructions Per Second): A measure of computer performance.

Mixdown: The process of combining the signals of several tracks to create a final mono or stereo version.

Monitor: A video display with composite or RGB video inputs. In audio, a personal amplifier and/or speaker system designed to emulate larger systems used in presentation or performance.

Monochrome: A display or printer producing only black and white images. Some monochrome monitors use other colors (e.g., green) instead of white.

Mono (Monophonic): An audio signal that has one channel of information.

MS-DOS (Microsoft Disk Operating System): The

operating system designed for the IBM and IBM compatible personal computers.

Muti-image: A slide show that uses two or more slide projectors in a programmed presentation.

Multimedia: The integration of video, graphics and audio through the computer.

Multiscan Monitor: A video monitor that works at various scan frequencies allowing it to be used with different graphics adapters.

Multi-screen: Projecting images onto several image areas.

Multi-tasking: An operating system that can run more than one program a a time.

Multitrack: A recording method in which more than two tracks are used to record individual portions of an audio production.

Noise: In audio, it is electrical interference or unwanted sound. In video this interference appears as "snow."

NTSC (National Television Standard Committee): An advisory group to the FCC that sets the standards for video hardware and broadcasting. The US standard is 525 lines per frame, interlaced, with 30 frames per second.

OCR: Optical Character Reader (or recognizer.)

Omnidirectional Microphone: Accepts sound equally well from all directions.

Optical Disk: A storage medium that records and reproduces digital information using a laser beam.

OS/2: A Microsoft multitasking operating system with virtual memory that allows a system to run networks.

OSF/MOTIF: A graphical user interface that provides standards for a wide range of computing environments.

Out-point: Where an edit ends. Also called end-point.

Overdubbing: The process of adding additional musical parts to previously recorded tracks.

Overscan: Computer screen mode that extends a computer graphics image to the limits of the visible TV screen.

PAL (Phase Alternating Line): The video standard used in Western Europe, Latin America, Great Britain, South Africa, Australia; not compatible with NTSC.

Palette: The selection of colors available in a computer graphics system.

Pan: A camera move that swings along the horizontal axis.

Pan Pot (Panoramic Potentiometer): Two connected

volume controls for left and right channels in a stereo mix wired so that one level increases as the other decreases.

Parts: The performances of individual instruments or vocalists that make up a composition.

Patch: Connecting video and audio equipment with cables or through a central panel.

Peripheral: An input or output device connected to the computer. Includes printers, plotters, file servers, terminals, CD-ROM's, laser videodisks, etc.

Phone Plug/Socket: A two or three lead connector standard based on a 1/4" diameter plug element found in the microphone inputs and headphones of most consumer-grade audio equipment. This connector also exists in mini- and micro- sizes.

Phono Plug/Socket: A two-lead connector system for shielded cables sometimes called RCA connectors. This connector is used for both video and audio signals on most consumer products.

Pixel: The basic picture element of a computer screen or digital graphics device. The smallest dot a computer can generate.

Pixelization: Using image processing software to break up a continuous image into rectangular blocks to give it a digitized look.

Post-production: Any process that takes place after the

shooting – editing, audio sweetening, or adding special effects and graphics.

POV (Point Of View): The viewing angle and apparent position of the camera.

Pre-roll: Rewinding tape in an editing VCR to a cue point so the tape is up to speed when rolled forward to the editing point.

Presentation Manager: A graphical user interface built into OS/2.

Raster Graphics: A graphics system in which the computer image is treated as a collection of dots.

Real-time Animation: The ability to create and display animation at the final viewing speed.

Rear Screen Projection: Projection of an image onto a translucent screen material for viewing from the opposite side. The screen is between the projector and the viewer.

Reference Black Level (Pedestal): Part of the video signal that provides a reference level for total picture brightness.

Resolution: The clarity or graininess of a video or computer image as measured by lines or pixels; the smallest resolvable detail in an image.

Reverberation (Reverb): The persistence of sound in a physical environment.

Reverse Video: Dark characters on a light background.

RGB (Red, Green, Blue): The primary colors of light which are mixed to provide any desired hue in a video image. RGB video keeps the intensity of each of these three colors on separate cables to produce higher quality images than available with composite video. RGB video output can be either analog or digital.

RGB Monitor: A type of color monitor with separate inputs for red, green and blue. It is especially well suited for high resolution color images.

Routing: The process of controlling the path taken by an audio signal.

Sample: A digitized version of a sound as processed by a sampler.

Sampler: An audio device that converts sound to digital information that can be manipulated by a computer. Many high quality music synthesizers use sampled sounds from acoustic instruments as the basis for their signals.

Saturation: The intensity of a particular hue.

Scan Converter: A device that changes the scan rate of a video signal, and may also convert it from interlaced to non-interlaced mode. This allows computer graphics to be displayed on a standard video screen.

Scan Rate: The speed with which the electron beam scans the picture tube.

Screen Dump: To send a picture on the display screen to the printer.

Screen Printer: A printer that accepts video input and produces a monochrome or color picture directly.

Screen Shot: A photograph of the screen of a computer or video monitor.

Sequencer: Software for controlling MIDI musical devices.

Shotgun: A cardioid microphone that picks up sound only in a narrow cone in front of the microphone.

Signal Path: The complete route followed by a signal in a recording system.

Signal Processor: Any device used to change an audio signal. Common examples are equalizers, mixers, compressors and reverberation units.

Signal to Noise Ratio: A measurement of noise introduced in an audio component expressed as the difference in decibels between the desired signal and the unwanted noise.

Single Screen: A presentation in which all the images are superimposed on the same screen area.

Slide-show Option: A feature offered by some presentation software products that allows slides to be shown on the computer screen in a predetermined order.

SMPTE (Society of Motion Picture and Television Engineers): An organization that sets technical standards for film and video.

SMPTE Time Code: An eight-digit address code used to identify each videotape frame by hour, minute, second and frame number for precise editing.

Song Position Pointer: A MIDI message that indicates the measure number and quarter-note beat location within a composition.

Special Effects Generator: A device used to produce wipes, split screens, inserts, keys and mattes.

Split Screen: A video effect that shows images from two different video sources, each on one half of the screen. Multiple split screens show images from several sources or different actions taking place in several windows in the screen area.

Stair-stepping: Refers to discontinuous nature of a line drawn at any angle other than horizontal or vertical. Also called "jaggies."

Stereo (Stereophonic): An audio signal that has two channels of information meant to be reproduced on two separate loudspeakers.

Still-frame Storage Unit: A digital device used to store individual video frames, any of which can be recalled for display.

Still Video: A camera that stores still images on magnetic disks rather than on film.

Storyboard: A visual outline of the narrative of a video production.

Striping: The process of recording a sync tone, or time code, onto a track of tape.

Subcarrier: The portion of the composite video signal containing the color information.

Superimposition: Laying titles or graphics over a video image.

S-VHS (Super VHS): Videotape format that provides for better resolution and less noise than standard VHS tapes.

Sweetening: Audio post-production, with an emphasis on adjusting the content for the best quality.

Switcher: A device for instantly controlling two or more video signals to create special patterns such as dissolves, wipes and keys.

Synchronization (Sync): The process of linking devices to play in an exact time relationship to one another.

Sync Generator: A device that generates the sync pulses used by all the components in a video system.

Sync Tone: An audio tone that encodes clock or time information in a form that can be read by a sequencer or other device.

Synthesizer (Synth): An electronic device for creating musical sounds and sound effects.

Talking Head: Slang for the typical head and shoulders shot of actors used on newscasts and talk shows. This is the worst possible format for instructional video.

Tape Format: Any of several tape widths and recording methods, such as 1/2" VHS and 3/4" U-Matic used in video recording.

TIFF (Tag Image File Format): The format used for transporting computerized versions of scanned images.

Time Base: The timing portion of a video signal, particularly the horizontal and vertical sync pulses.

Time Base Corrector (TBC): A device that corrects time-base signal instabilities caused by VCR's during playback making it possible for two or more VCR's to be in sync.

Time Code: An electronic counter or indicator of videotape duration; the hours, minutes, seconds, and frames that the tape lasts. This is usually visible only with a special time code reader.

Tint: Amount of white in the saturation of a color.

Track: The location or path of a recorded signal on a tape or disk.

Track Bouncing: A process by which multiple tracks are mixed and re-recorded onto another track for the purpose of freeing tracks for further recording.

Transport Controller: A computer device that controls the operation of a VCR with frame accuracy.

U-Matic: Trade name for the 3/4" videotape format invented by Sony.

UNIX: A multi-user, multi-tasking operating system edging its way into the personal computer realm.

Upload: To receive data from another computer by direct connection or through a modem.

VCR (Video Cassette Recorder): A device for recording video on cassettes.

VDA (Video Distribution Amplifier): A device used to allow the connection of several monitors to one video source.

Vector Graphics: A display technology that builds images from the strokes of lines rather than from collections of individual pixels.

Vectorscope: Video test equipment that displays information about the color portion of the video signal.

Vertical Blanking Interval: The time between fields from one vertical scan to the start of the next. Other information can be sent during this period.

Vertical Resolution: The number of pixels available vertically down the screen.

Vertical Scan Rate: The speed at which the electron beam scans down the entire screen of a monitor.

VGA (Video Graphics Adapter): High quality graphics standard for MS-DOS computers compatible with EGA; also supports analog monitors.

VHS (Video Home System): The most popular 1/2" consumer videotape format.

Videoconferencing: The ability for groups at distant locations to participate, through audio and video, in the same meeting at the same time.

Video Player: A device that only plays back, but does not record, videotapes or optical disks.

Video Signal: A waveform carrying video information.

Videospace: The sum total of all the visual elements that interact to create the visual counterpart to audiospace.

Video Still Camera: A camera generally shaped like a 35 mm film camera that captures still images and saves them on magnetic disks in an analog video format. Consumer grade devices capture single fields, and professional grade cameras can capture fields and frames. This technology also allows for up to 10 seconds of audio to be captured along with each picture.

Virtual Reality: Highly realistic computer simulations that use 3-dimensional displays to create the impression of being inside a place.

Virtual Tracks: Parts played by a sequencer during final mixdown as if they were being played from a tape deck.

Waveform Monitor: Video test equipment that measures and displays the parameters of the video signal.

Windows: A graphical user interface for IBM and compatible personal computers.

Wipe: A visual transition in which one image replaces another along a border that moves across the screen.

WYSIWYG (What You See Is What You Get): The image on the computer display screen corresponds exactly to the printed output.

XLR: An audio connector that uses three pins. This connector is often used with cables designed to allow low level signals to be carried long distances without picking up noise. XLR connectors are often found on semi-professional and professional audio components.

References:

Thomas Armstrong, *In Their Own Way*, J. P. Tarcher, 1987.
Mihaly Csikszentmihalyi, *Beyond Boredom and Anxiety*, Jossey-Bass, 1975.
Mihaly and Isabella Csikszentmihalyi, *Flow: The Psychology of Optimal Experience*, Harper and Row, 1990.
Stanley Davis, *Future Perfect*, Addison-Wesley, 1987.
Howard Gardner, *Frames of Mind*, Basic Books, 1983.
William Glasser, *The Quality School: Managing Students Without Coercion*, Harper and Row, 1990.
Leslie Hart, *Human Brain and Human Learning*, Brain Age Publishers, 1983.
Andy LePage, *Transforming Education*, Oakmore House, 1987.
Dudley Lynch and Paul Kordis, *Strategy of the Dolphin: Scoring a Win in a Chaotic World*, Fawcett, 1988.
Tom Peters, *Thriving on Chaos: Handbook for Management Revolution*, Alfred Knopf, 1988.
Neil Postman, *Amusing Ourselves to Death: Public Discourse in the Age of Show Business*, Penguin Books, 1985.
Bob Samples, *Open Mind/Whole Mind*, Jalmar Press, 1987.
David Thornburg, *Chaotic Microworlds: Personal Computing and the Art of Mathematics*, Starsong Publications, 1990.
Alvin Toffler, *Powershift – Knowledge, Wealth and Violence at the Edge of the 21st Century*, Bantam Books, 1990.